SpringerBriefs in Economics

SpringerBriefs present concise summaries of cutting-edge research and practical applications across a wide spectrum of fields. Featuring compact volumes of 50 to 125 pages, the series covers a range of content from professional to academic. Typical topics might include:

- A timely report of state-of-the art analytical techniques
- A bridge between new research results, as published in journal articles, and a contextual literature review
- A snapshot of a hot or emerging topic
- An in-depth case study or clinical example
- A presentation of core concepts that students must understand in order to make independent contributions

SpringerBriefs in Economics showcase emerging theory, empirical research, and practical application in microeconomics, macroeconomics, economic policy, public finance, econometrics, regional science, and related fields, from a global author community.

Briefs are characterized by fast, global electronic dissemination, standard publishing contracts, standardized manuscript preparation and formatting guidelines, and expedited production schedules.

Alessia Berni

The Complex Environments of Special Economic Zones

Challenges and Opportunities in Italy

Springer

Alessia Berni
Department of Business and Economics
Parthenope University of Naples
Naples, Italy

ISSN 2191-5504 ISSN 2191-5512 (electronic)
SpringerBriefs in Economics
ISBN 978-3-031-83424-0 ISBN 978-3-031-83425-7 (eBook)
https://doi.org/10.1007/978-3-031-83425-7

This Springer imprint is published by the registered company Springer Nature Switzerland AG
The registered company address is: Gewerbestrasse 11, 6330 Cham, Switzerland

This book is dedicated to Alice

Preface

This work provides valuable insights into the use of special economic zones (SEZs) as a powerful instrument for stimulating investment, creating employment opportunities, and supporting economic growth through tax incentives and other economic benefits. Institutional actors commit to offering efficient processes and ample resources in a highly competitive setting to foster the advancement of global and economic markets. Developing nations commonly use SEZs as a tool to stimulate development and foster economic growth. This book is the result of research and studies undertaken in the organisational domain of Special Economic Zones in recent years. The project, titled "Research on Crisis areas, SEZ, and the Work Plan in Campania," involved collaboration among universities across the region to support the Campania Region in the formulation and execution of Special Economic Zones. The research group at the University of Parthenope contributed to the project by concentrating their investigation on organisational issues. Firstly, I wish to express my gratitude to the several scholars whose work inspired my writing. This work would not have been achievable without the support and discussions of colleagues from the University of Naples Parthenope, Vanvitelli University, University of Naples Federico II, University of Sannio, University of Molise, and University of Salerno.

My greatest gratitude goes out to Luigi Moschera, who has played a crucial role in my academic career for nearly twenty years. His guidance, understanding, and support have been essential in my development as a much stronger researcher. Živilė Stankevičiūtė and Vincenza Esposito for their outstanding help during the review process.

Finally, I want to thank everyone who helped me at different points during the manuscript's draughting process.

For his kindness and help, I am very grateful to Niko Chtouris of Springer Briefs.

Naples, Italy

Alessia Berni

Competing Interests

The author has no competing interests to declare that are relevant to the content of this manuscript.

Contents

Chapter 1
Special Economic Zones: Goals and Definitions

1.1 Introduction

This work provides valuable insights into the use of Special Economic Zones (SEZs) as a powerful instrument for stimulating investment, creating employment opportunities, and supporting economic growth through tax incentives and other economic benefits. Institutional actors commit to offering efficient processes and ample resources in a highly competitive setting to foster the advancement of global and economic markets. Developing nations commonly use SEZs as a tool to stimulate development and foster economic growth. While most studies primarily examine the economic consequences of Special Economic Zones (SEZ), there is a dearth of research that explores the influence of other factors, such as management, governance, stakeholder involvement, and institutional framework, on the advancement of these regions. Therefore, examining the role of actors and the governance mechanism in the network from its inception is fascinating. Global evidence suggests that the interactions of various institutional entities (such as national and local governments, agencies, public and commercial organisations, etc.) are crucial to fostering innovation, promoting development, and enhancing competitiveness.

1.2 Research Aim

Over the past few years, this work has been one of the results of research and studies conducted in the organisational domain of special economic zones (Berni & Moschera, 2019, 2020, 2021; Maryami et al., 2019). Among the others, I have been a member of the research group within the project 'Research on crisis areas, SEZ, and the work plan in Campania', which involved the collaboration of universities throughout the region to assist the Campania Region in the design and

A. Berni, *The Complex Environments of Special Economic Zones*,
SpringerBriefs in Economics, https://doi.org/10.1007/978-3-031-83425-7_1

implementation of the Special Economic Zones. The University of Parthenope's research group contributed to the initiative by focusing its analysis on organisational issues and, conversely, labour economics (Berni & Moschera, 2021; Ciociano et al., 2020a, b).

The primary goal of this book is to provide a comprehensive overview of Special Economic Zones from an organisational perspective. Therefore, it aims to focus on organisational and governance issues related to these special areas.

The objective is to examine, firstly, the different types of special areas, and secondly, their impact on the economy and the workforce.

During the preliminary phase, we reviewed the relevant literature on the subject. The most relevant studies and research on networks and related governance models have been analysed. Apart from academic articles, reports and articles from international organisations as an additional bibliographic source have also been consulted. We specifically examined publications from the World Bank, UNIDO (United Nations Industrial Development Organization), the Facility for Investment Climate Advisory Services (FIAS), the ILO, and documents released by various authorities managing special economic zones around the world.

The work continued in a second phase with an analysis of the relevant international experiences. A review of the cases on a geographic basis has been conducted, deemed most pertinent for analysis, aiming to enhance comprehension of the existing experiences in the international arena.

In 2019, the research group conducted a thorough analysis of the SEZ situation in Italy. They found that, in accordance with the law decree of June 20, 2017, no. 91 (which was later transformed by Law n.123, 3 August 2017 n. 123), the regional strategic plans of the affected regions had indeed incorporated the SEZ proposals, with a particular focus on the Campania region. Later, the legislative framework has changed. The regulation establishing Special Economic Zones (SEZ) was implemented with the DPCM of January 25, 2018 (GURI General Series No. 47 of February 26, 2018).

The Decree of the Director General of the Agency (4/2023), which completely supersedes No. 69/2022, regulates the complex 'Supporto ZES' Italian project.

Decree-Law No. 124/2023 establishes the 'ZES unica', the Special Economic Zone for the Mezzogiorno, effective January 1, 2024. This zone encompasses the territories of the regions of Abruzzo, Basilicata, Calabria, Campania, Molise, Puglia, Sicily, and Sardinia, and it replaces the current fragmented Special Economic Zones within eight distinct administrative structures.

The economic framework and labour market play an important role in expanding, updating, and deepening the regional context analysis. This contribution tries to address the issue of SEZ from various perspectives with the aim of providing some strategic indications regarding alternative intervention methodologies and tools.

Considering these reflections and considerations, the volume is organised into four chapters.

The initial chapter provides an overview of the Special Economic Zones and the underlying rationale for the work's development. The chapter focuses on the primary definitions of the subject under investigation and the objectives of the research.

In addition, a literature review on SEZs is beneficial to illustrate the way institutional connections between organisations develop and establish a framework for evaluating the intricate management system. Many studies have investigated SEZs with an emphasis on economic elements, even though few have examined governance.

The second chapter focuses on policy and organisational concerns. The objective of this section is to establish a framework for the Special Economic Zones instrument, which will describe the inter-organisational relationships and forms of collaboration among academic institutions, industrial organisations, researchers, policymakers, and institutional actors who are involved in a joint project to promote regional development. The goal is to present a comprehensive overview of the current state of Special Economic Zones (SEZ), beginning with their objectives and global distribution and proceeding to an analysis of the primary governance models.

The third chapter investigates the government models and regulations that oversee special economic zones on a global scale. To ascertain policies and best practices that can inform the development of work policies and governance structures for new SEZs, this contribution analyses numerous international special zone activations.

The final chapter pertains to special economic zones (SEZs) in Italy. The emergence and development of special economic zones in Italy will be the focus of this section. The implementation of a special zone as a complex intervention area to promote economic growth in underdeveloped or transitioning areas, such as the South Central, is an innovative approach, even though regions with similar features that are included in the SEZ or are subject to a special tax regime are not innovative to Italy.

1.3 Special Economic Zones: A Literature Overview[1]

Although the term 'Special Economic Zone' has several definitions, in general, it refers to specific geographical areas within a country that adhere to more liberal trade and employment laws than the common regulations in the rest of the country (OECD, 2017; Zeng, 2015). Generally, we classify special economic zones based on their primary economic objectives. The different zones can be classified into six main modern zones: export processing zones, free trade zones, enterprise zones, freeports, single factory zones, and specialised zones (Akinci & Crittle, 2008). In this study, we expand our analysis to include export processing zones, free trade zones, freeports, and high-tech parks, considering the World Bank's classification, the geographical circumstances of the case studies, and the unique characteristics of each country's zones. Examining the history of studies on special economic zones

[1] This paragraph includes a few of the considerations that have been made in previous research studies on the subject (Berni and Moschera (2020, 2021) and Maryami et al. (2019)).

reveals that most studies have investigated SEZs with an emphasis on economic elements, even though few have examined governance models, network, management policies, or network approach as a distinct approach to improving the efficacy of these special regions.

Since the end of the 1990s, a great number of academics have produced publications that are pertinent to SEZ. In particular, I carried out a database search and discovered almost 250 articles that pertain to the business sector. By narrowing the scope of the investigation and concentrating just on the articles that are pertinent to my study objective (management and governance networks), the number of articles that were published in the business area journal between the years 1991 and 2024 is reduced to fewer than eighty.

Despite the existence of similar works, numerous researchers have compared SEZs to gain a deeper understanding. Therefore, the outcome will offer policymakers in special economic zones a variety of innovative processes to enhance the efficiency of both the public and private sectors operating within them. By considering the critical role of SEZs in attracting investors, literature reviews highlighted the studies that focus on the relationship between SEZs' performance and their ability to attract FDI (Chakraborty et al., 2017; Chandrachud & Gajalakshmi, 2013). There are a considerable number of studies that focus on the impact of different types of SEZs on the economic growth of host countries (Akinci & Crittle, 2008; Sinenko & Mayburov, 2017; Zeng, 2016; Frazier, 2018). Another characteristic of SEZs is their analysis, particularly in relation to the economic conditions of developing countries (Hakimian, 2011; Kuzmenko et al., 2018; Yeung et al., 2009). Comparative studies on the main capacity of Special Economic Zones (SEZs) in promoting economic growth are noteworthy across various research domains. These studies highlight the more successful zones in India, China, and African countries (Farole, 2011; Le Roux & Schoeman, 2016; Wu, 2018; Zeng, 2015). The background of studies on special economic zones reveals that most of them focus on analysing the economic aspects of these zones. Consequently, only a few types of research have tackled the governing structure (Chen, 1995; Grubel, 1982; Moberg, 2015; Williamson, 1991) or management policy in these zones (Malhotra & Papadopoulos, 2008). The result will provide a range of innovative processes for policymakers in special economic zones to improve the effective operations of public and private sectors in these zones. In recent years, the focus has primarily been on expanding practical awareness about the institutional structure of SEZs and investigating the impact of the political situation on the performance efficiency of these zones. In their study, Farole and Kweka (2011) adjusted the instructional practices in Tanzania. They examined various institutional and administrative structures for managing an SEZ program, highlighting effective strategies for success in the zones, as well as the reasons for the plan's failure in these zones in Tanzania. Zeng (2015), focusing on the global experience of SEZs, concludes that the success of these special zones hinges on the design of legal and regulatory frameworks and the application of strategic planning. Hazakis (2014) focused on the rationale behind SEZs, examining the existing literature on SEZs' institutional approaches.

1.3.1 The Policy Network Approach to Study SEZs

In the light of these considerations, it is worth illustrating the way institutional connections between organisations develop and establishing a framework for evaluating the intricate management system. SEZ outlines relationships and collaborations between academic institutions, industrial organisations, researchers, policymakers, and institutional actors involved in a shared project to promote regional development. The type of collaboration and the interconnections between public and private entities are crucial in generating value, fostering regional advancement, and facilitating economic expansion. In light of this, authorities are taking steps to promote initiatives that stimulate innovation and streamline the creation and exchange of knowledge.

Based on a network policy approach, an organisation is considered as part of a complex arrangement that has multiple interactions with other organisations and sectors. The level and quality of inter-organisational relationships and partnerships are influenced by a set of factors such as the level of trust and commitment and similarity in their target and approaches for participation in partnership. Boerzel (1997) defined the policy networks as a network of actors who benefit from determining the policy, providing resources (material and non-material) for adjusting, deciding, and implementing these politics and exchanging information by organising communications with each other in a network structure. They provide mechanisms for cooperation between groups and institutions and define their working conditions not just in terms of intrinsic characteristics but by describing their relationship with other contributors. As Rhodes (2009, p. 426) defines it: 'Policy networks are sets of formal institutional and informal linkages between governmental and other actors structured around shared, if endlessly negotiated, beliefs and interests in public policy-making and implementation'.

The policy network approach is designed to provide the scheme for determining the complex processes to develop management processes and strategies, and it illustrates the framework for strategic interaction processes and institutional relations in organisations (Klijn & Koppenjan, 2000).

Moberg (2015) in his study investigated the political economy of Special Economic Zones to highlight the efficient mechanism that can improve the capacities of an SEZ model by analysing the institutions that channel information and incentives of officials and businesses. He discussed that a robust political economy framework can help policymakers to understand which institutions can improve an SEZ program.

According to differences in concepts of network policy in literature of studies, Klijn (1996) classified the background of different studies on public policy in three features: dependency, process, and institutions. Pedersen (2010), by analysing case studies of decision-making processes in two Danish land-use projects in the wider countryside, asserted that the weak network can sometimes prove to be the more powerful of the two networks regarding specific project decisions. Farole and Moberg (2014) investigated the political economy challenge in special economy zones by proposing a 'robust political economy' framework that divides political economy problems into those of inadequate knowledge and distorted incentives by reviewing African special economic zones.

Papadopoulou et al. (2011) examined rural development projects with respect to their structural and politico-administrative dimensions, including power relations, conflicts, multi-functionality, and intersectorality in Greece.

The policy network approach is used to study policy-making processes (Dowding, 1995; Moberg, 2015) and network governance (Vollenberg et al., 2007). Public management and policy networks (Borzel, 1997) and privatisation and corporate governance (Martinez et al., 2013) have been studied further.

By making use of the framework, it is possible to evaluate the significance of the policy network approach to the administration of special economic zones and investigate the organisational structures.

References

Akinci, G., & Crittle, J. (2008). *Special economic zone: Performance, lessons learned, and implication for zone development* (Vol. No. 45869, pp. 1–83). The World Bank. The Multi Donor Investment Climate Advisory Service. April.

Berni, A., & Moschera, L. (2019). Dealing with complex environments: The case of special economic zones in Italy. In *Knowledge ecosystems and growth: 14th international forum on knowledge asset dynamics - IFKAD 2019*. ISBN: 978-88-96687-12-3.

Berni, A., & Moschera, L. (2020). La Sfida Della Complessità: Le Zone Economiche Speciali In Italia. In L. Moschera & F. E. Caroleo (Eds.), *Le Zone Economiche Speciali: Aspetti Organizzativi E Di Policy. Vol. Annals Of Crisei* (Vol. 2). ISBN: 978-88-98279-10-4.

Berni, A., & Moschera, L. (2021). La Letteratura Su Policy Network e modelli di governance. In AA. VV (Ed.), *R. Realfonzo, Le politiche per lo sviluppo in Campania ZES, piano del lavoro, aree di crisi* (pp. 43–58). UNIOR Press. ISBN: 978-88-6719-201-4.

Borzel, T. A. (1997). *Organizing Babylon: on the different conceptions of policy networks*. Public Administration.

Chakraborty, T., Gundimeda, H., & Kathuria, V. (2017). Have the special economic zones succeeded in attracting FDI? Analysis for India. *Theoretical Economics Letters, 7*, 623–642.

Chandrachud, S., & Gajalakshmi, P. (2013). A study on role of FDI in SEZ - special reference to MEPZ. *International Journal of Business and Management Invention, 2*, 3.

Chen, X. (1995). The evolution of free economic zones and the recent development of cross-national growth zones. *International Journal of Urban and Regional Research, 19*(4), 593–621.

Ciociano, E., Berni, A., & Moschera, L. (2020a). Modelli Di Governance E Politiche Per Il Lavoro: Le Zone Economiche Speciali Nel Mondo. In L. Moschera & F. E. Caroleo (Eds.), *Le Zone Economiche Speciali: Aspetti Organizzativi E Di Policy. Vol. Annals Of Crisei* (Vol. 2). ISBN: 978-88-98279-10-4.

Ciociano, E., De Iudicibus, A., & Berni, A. (2020b). Analisi Della Governance E Delle Politiche Del Lavoro: Proposte Per Il Caso Campano. In L. Moschera & F. E. Caroleo (Eds.), *Le Zone Economiche Speciali: Aspetti Organizzativi E Di Policy. Vol. Annals Of Crisei* (Vol. 2). ISBN: 978-88-98279-10-4.

Dowding, K. (1995). Model or metaphor? A critical review of the policy network approach. *Political Science Journal, 43*(1).

Farole, T. (2011). *Special economic zones in Africa. Comparing performance and learning from global experiences. Directions in development—Trade, n. 60059*. The World Bank.

Farole, T., & Kweka, J. (2011). *Institutional best practices for special economic zones: An application to Tanzania - Africa Trade Policy Note*. siteresources.worldbank.org
Farole, T., & Moberg, L. (2014). *It worked in China, so why not in Africa? The political economy challenge of Special Economic Zones* (No. 2014/152). WIDER Working Paper.
Frazier, M. (2018). Emergence of a new Hanseatic league: How special economic zones will reshape global governance. *Chapman Law Review, 21*, 333.
Grubel, H. G. (1982). Towards a theory of free economic zones. *Welt wirtschaftliches Archive, 118*(1), 39.
Hakimian, H. (2011). Iran's free trade zones: Back doors to the international economy? *Iranian Studies, 44*(6), 851–874.
Hazakis, K. J. (2014). The rationale of special economic zones (SEZs): An institutional approach. *Regional Science Policy & Practice, 6*(1), 85–101.
Klijn, E. (1996). Analyzing and managing policy processes in complex networks: A theoretical examination of the concept policy network and its problems. *Administration & Society, 28*(1), 90–119.
Klijn, E. H., & Koppenjan, J. F. (2000). Public management and policy networks: Foundations of a network approach to governance. *Public Management an International Journal of Research and Theory, 2*(2), 135–158.
Kuzmenko, O. A., Pelkova, S. V., Lukianenko, O. V., & Fomichev, I. Y. (2018). Comparative analysis of taxation for special economic zones in Russia and APEC economies. *European Research Studies Journal, XXI*. Special Issue 1.
Le Roux, N., & Schoeman, A. (2016). A comparative analysis of the design of special economic zones: The case of South Africa, Malaysia and Indonesia. *Journal of Economic and Financial Sciences, 9*(3), 749–768.
Malhotra, S., & Papadopoulos, N. (2008). A comparative analysis of investment climate at free trade zones and host country mainland. *ASAC, 29*(8).
Martinez, M., Jamison, M., & Tillmar, M. (2013). Public utilities corporate governance. *Journal of Management & Governance, 17*(4), 827–833.
Maryami, S., Pezzillo, I. M., Martinez, M., & Berni, A. (2019). Special economic zones' governance and organizational structures: A comparative study on a policy network approach in Iran, UAE and Kazakhstan. In *Knowledge ecosystems and growth: IFKAD 2019*. ISBN: 978-88-96687-12-3.
Moberg, L. (2015). The political economy of special economic zones. *Journal of Institutional Economics, 11*(1), 167–190.
OECD. (2017). *Tracking special economic zones in the Western Balkans: objectives, features and key challenges*, http://www.oecd.org/south-east-europe/special-economic-zones.htm
Papadopoulou, E., Hasanagas, N., & Harvey, D. (2011). Analysis of rural development policy networks in Greece: Is LEADER really different? *Land Use Policy, 28*(4), 663–673.
Pedersen, A. B. (2010). Why David sometimes defeats goliath: The power of actors in disprivileged land-use policy networks. *Land Use Policy, 27*(2), 324–331.
Rhodes, R. A. W. (2009). *Policy Network Analysis*. The Oxford Handbook of Public Policy. 28. https://doi.org/10.1093/oxfordhb/9780199548453.003.0020
Sinenko, O., & Mayburov, I. (2017). Comparative analysis of the effectiveness of special economic zones and their influence on the development of territories. *International Journal of Economics and Financial Issues, 7*(1), 115–122.
Vollenberg, M., Kenis, P., & Raab, J. (2007). Provan and Milward 1995 revisited: A case-study on network structure and network effectiveness of a Dutch mental health care network. In *9th Public Management Research Conference, Tucson, Arizona October*.
Williamson, O. E. (1991). Strategizing, economizing, and economic organization. *Strategic Management Journal, 12*(S2), 75–94.
Wu, W. (2018). *Pioneering economic reform in China's special economic zones: The promotion of foreign investment and technology transfer in Shenzhen*. Routledge.

Yeung, E., Lee, J., & Kee, G. (2009). China's special economic zones at 30. *Eurasian Geography and Economics., 50*(2), 222–240.

Zeng, D. Z. (2015). *Global experiences with special economic zones: focus on China and Africa.* World Bank Policy Research Working Paper (7240).

Zeng, D. Z. (2016). *Special Economic Zones: Lessons from the Global Experience.* PEDL - Private Enterprise Development in Low Income Countries PEDL Synthesis Paper Series n. 1.

Chapter 2
Special Economic Zones: A Policy and Organisational Analysis

2.1 Introduction

This paragraph aims to establish a structure for understanding the concept of special economic zones. It describes relationships and collaborations among academic institutions, industrial organisations, researchers, policymakers, and institutional actors who are working together on a project to promote regional development. The objective is to assess the status of Special Economic Zones (SEZs), beginning with their goals and global distribution and subsequently examining the primary governance types.[1]

The performance of the SEZ can be affected by both the governance model chosen and the labour policies implemented in the special area. By examining the practices of special areas implemented globally, we can identify the advantages and disadvantages of the governance models, policies, and actions used to tackle labour market challenges in areas with Special Economic Zones (SEZs) that are created or intended to promote employment growth (Berni & Moschera, 2021).

The forms of collaboration and relationships between public and private entities are pivotal in generating value, fostering regional advancement, and facilitating economic expansion. Considering this, authorities are taking steps to promote initiatives that stimulate innovation and aid in the creation and dissemination of knowledge. Institutional players, in a fiercely competitive setting, dedicate themselves to providing regulations and resources that promote the global and economic marketplace. From this perspective, developing nations frequently employ the SEZ as a means for fostering development and promoting economic expansion.

Lately, academics and researchers have shown a growing interest in the establishment of special economic zones (SEZs) as an effective means to enhance

[1] This paragraph contains a summary of various research studies published on the topic (Berni and Moschera (2021) and Maryami et al. (2019)).

A. Berni, *The Complex Environments of Special Economic Zones*,
SpringerBriefs in Economics, https://doi.org/10.1007/978-3-031-83425-7_2

investments, promote employment, and facilitate economic growth by offering tax incentives and economic advantages (Akinci & Crittle, 2008). International evidence indicates that the collaboration between various institutional stakeholders (such as national and local governments, agencies, public and commercial organisations, etc.) is crucial for fostering innovation, promoting development, and strengthening competitiveness (Sun & Cao, 2018). While most studies primarily examine the economic consequences of the SEZ, a smaller proportion of research delves into the influence of other factors, such as management and governance, the roles of actors, and the institutional framework, on the effectiveness of these special areas. Therefore, it is intriguing to examine the actors' function and the governance mechanism in the network from its beginning.

2.2 Definitions of Special Economic Zones

The number of free trade zones is experiencing rapid and significant growth. While the concept of free zones dates to roughly 1700, there has been a significant global expansion in the number of special economic zones in the past two decades. In 1997, the number of these entities was 845, spread across 93 nations. However, by 2016, the number had increased to approximately 4500, spanning across 135 countries. Asia accounted for 43% of these, while Europe accounted for 20%. As of 2019, there has been a continuous increase in the number of Special Economic Zones (SEZs) globally, reaching a total of 5383 SEZs. Notably, Asia accounts for 75.2% of these SEZs (UNCTAD, 2019).

The Special Economic Zones (SEZ) aim to facilitate the growth of current firms and the foundation of new enterprises in certain locations by creating advantageous economic, financial, and administrative conditions. To summarise, we can categorise the distinctive attributes that, when reinterpreted in a unique manner, establish a special economic zone into three domains (Table 2.1).

Table 2.1 SEZ characteristics. *Source*: Adapted from Vats et al. (2018)

Incentives	It offers direct financial benefits to companies or individuals operating in the SEZ, attracting businesses and residents, and fostering rapid economic growth in the SEZ Examples include reduced tariffs, taxes, or duties, repatriation of profits, refunds, or subsidies, investment and financing options
Regulation	It offers special regulation It facilitates autonomy and creates an attractive location Examples include a dedicated regulatory authority, a regulatory framework based on international standards, and regulatory transparency
Operation	It offers infrastructure and services to support industrial, commercial, and residential activities Attracts talent to offer quality services Examples include high-quality communication infrastructure, specialised laboratories, consulting services, and integrated public transport

Table 2.2 SEZ: direct and indirect benefits

Direct economic benefits	Indirect economic benefits
Creation of new job opportunities	Skill enhancement
Expansion of international trade	Transfer and technical advancement
Increase in government revenue	Export diversification
Increase in foreign direct investments	Effectiveness of local businesses is improved.
Rise in foreign currency earnings	Urban and regional development
	Enhancement of industrial clusters

The establishment of special economic zones offers significant advantages, in terms of both direct and indirect economic benefits (Table 2.2).

Literature employs an extensive and diverse vocabulary to delineate the notion of special economic zones. Generally, they represent specific geographical areas within a nation where unique regulations govern commercial activities, setting them apart from the rest of the economy. Businesses choose to establish themselves in these places due to the presence of incentives or economic advantages.

The fundamental concept of the SEZ is comprehensive and can encompass several specific attributes outlined below:

a) a geographically delineated region typically characterised by physical barriers for protection.
b) a singular direction or governance.
c) Provides benefits to investors who are geographically situated inside the region.
d) It possesses an independent customs zone where duties are imposed without any associated benefits, along with streamlined processes (Akinci & Crittle, 2008; Farole, 2011).

Moreover, these regions boast a comprehensive system of instruments, motivations, and streamlined administrative procedures that frequently diverge from the country's current legislation. Unido (2015) designed this system to increase the appeal of the Special Economic Zones to foreign investors. Specifically, within the framework of the Italian legal system, the precise definition of a Special Economic Zone (SEZ) pertains to a designated territory that possesses distinct features. As per the decree law of June 20, 2017, no. 91, known as the 'Urgent provisions for economic growth in the Mezzogiorno', an SEZ is defined as a specific and clearly identified area within the borders of the State. It may include non-contiguous areas if they are economically connected and must have at least one port area that meets the requirements set by Regulation (EU) no. 1315 of December 11, 2013, of the European Parliament and of the Council, which outlines guidelines for the development of the trans-European transport network (TEN-T). Existing and future companies engaged in economic and entrepreneurial activities can benefit from favourable conditions specifically designed to foster investment growth and company development within the SEZ.

To effectively describe the SEZ, it is helpful to provide a concise summary of the diverse definitions of the different sorts of zones.

2.2.1 *Special Economic Zone (SEZ)*

The Special Economic Zone (SEZ) is a specific geographical area that implements a comprehensive set of measures, incentives, and administrative simplifications. These measures often deviate from the regulations applicable in the rest of the country, with the aim of making the SEZ more appealing to foreign investors (Akinci & Crittle, 2008; UNIDO, 2015).

2.2.2 *Free Trade Zones, Often Known As Free Trade Areas (FZ)*

One of the most common and earliest types of special zones in historical documentation is the free trade zone. A free trade zone is a designated region, typically smaller than 50 ha, that has a specific connection with airports and ports. The port authority typically oversees these zones, which are exempt from customs taxes. The port authority strategically positions these zones around key transportation hubs. Occasionally, they are physically constrained by the remaining space at the port because of the unique customs duty system concerning the national territory. The activities are restricted to trade-related procedures such as warehousing, storage, and sales, as well as processing operations including packaging, labelling, quality control, and sorting. One instance of this is the Colon Free Zone in Panama, as well as some zones formed in Iran and the United Arab Emirates (Akinci & Crittle, 2008).

2.2.3 *Export Processing Zones, Often Known As EPZs*

They are designated areas that are established by governments to promote and facilitate export-oriented industries. EPZs provide various incentives and benefits to attract foreign investment and encourage the production and export of goods and services. These are regions that offer incentives and unique benefits specifically for manufacturing operations and related industries, especially targeting overseas markets. The size of these regions is quite modest, with an area of less than 100 hectares. They provide firms with favourable trading circumstances and a less stringent regulatory environment, eliminating the necessity for them to demand a port or airport. Since the 1990s, the operations in these areas have experienced substantial diversification and expansion. There are two possible forms they can take.

The classic model of an Export Processing Zone (EPZ) is characterised by an exclusive area where only export-oriented firms that have been licensed under a particular regime can operate. The hybrid model consists of two distinct areas: one that is accessible to all enterprises, regardless of their focus on exporting, and another area exclusively designated for exporting companies registered in the special zone. Two classic examples are the Shannon export zone in Ireland and Karachi in Pakistan (Akinci & Crittle, 2008).

2.2.4 *Free Enterprise Zones, Also Known As Free Enterprise/ Single Factory Zones (FE)*

Their objective is to rejuvenate economically challenged urban or rural regions by offering tax incentives and financial assistance. They are predominantly located in developed nations, such as the United States, France, and the United Kingdom. One instance is the Empowerment Zone, located in Chicago. In certain instances, they can pertain exclusively to corporations or industries. These scenarios are commonly known as Single Factory EPZ Free Enterprises (FEs). In essence, Single Factory EPZ Free Enterprises (FEs) are a modified version of the EPZ concept, enabling a single corporation to obtain certain advantages.

2.2.5 *Free Ports, Also Known As Free Port Zones*

They are designated areas within a country where goods can be imported, stored, and processed without being subject to certain taxes and regulations that are often imposed on imports. Large areas, both in rural and urban settings, host a wide range of industries, including tourism and shopping (area larger than 100 km^2). There are numerous instances of this phenomenon in China, or one might go to the Aqaba region as a reference.

2.2.6 *Industrial Parks, Sometimes Known As IPs*

They are designated areas specifically designed and developed for industrial activities. Industrial parks, sometimes referred to as industrial zones, are primarily locations where production takes place and may provide a variety of incentives and advantages. Developed areas are split based on a functional design for roads, transport, and public utilities. These areas may or may not include advanced firms, but frequently provide incentives to support industrial groups (Unido, 2015).

2.2.7 *Eco-industrial Parks, Also Known As Eco-Industrial Park (EIP)*

Clusters of corporations, regions, or eco-industrial complexes prioritise ecological advancements by minimising waste and boosting the environmental efficacy of enterprises. They employ environmentally friendly technologies to attain energy efficiency and promote sustainability in their production processes. Due to the prevailing environmental concerns, a growing number of countries are adopting this novel form of designated area.

2.2.8 *Technological Parks, Often Known As Technology Parks (TPs)*

Experts lead these organisations, focusing on enhancing community welfare by cultivating a culture of innovation and competitiveness among the businesses they collaborate with. To accomplish these goals, the Science Park fosters and oversees the transfer of knowledge and technology between universities, research and development institutes, companies, and markets. It also facilitates the establishment and growth of innovative companies through incubation and spin-off processes. It provides additional value-added services alongside superior spaces and facilities.

Presented below are two tables that categorise SEZs based on their activity and market (Table 2.3) and their area of specialisation (Table 2.4).

Table 2.3 SEZs based on their activity and market. *Source*: Akinci and Crittle (2008)

Type of zone	Development objective	Physical configuration	Typical location	Eligible activities	Markets	Examples
Free trade zone (Commercial free zone)	Support trade	Size <50 ha	Parts of entry	Entrepôt and trade-related activities	Domestic, re-export	Colon free Zone, Panama
Traditional EPZ	Export manufacturing	Size <100 ha hectares Total area is designated as on EPZ	None	Manufacturing other processing	Mostly export	Karachi EPZ, Pakistan
Hybrid EPZ	Export manufacturing	Size <100 ha Only part of the area is designated as on EPZ	None	Manufacturing other processing	Export and domestic market	Lat Krabong Industrial Estate Thailand
Freeport	Integrated development	Size >00 Km^2	None	Multi-use	Domestic, internal, and export markets	Aqaba Special economic zone, Jordan
Enterprise zone, Empowerment, Urban free zones	Urban revitalisation	Size <50 ha	Distressed urban or rural areas	Multi-use	Domestic	Empowerment zone, Chicago
Single factory EPZ	Export manufacturing	Designation for individual enterprise	Countrywide	Manufacturing other processing	Export market	Mauritius Mexico Madagascar

Table 2.4 SEZs by area of specialisation. *Source*: Akinci and Crittle (2008)

Type of zone	Development objective	Size	Typical location	Activities	Markets	Examples
Technology or science parks	Promote high-tech and science-based industries	<50 ha	Adjacent to universities, institutes	High-technology activities	Domestic and export	Singapore Science Park, Singapore
Petrochemical zones	Promote energy industries	100–300 ha	Petrochemical hubs; efficient energy sources	Petrochemicals and other heavy industry	Domestic and export	Laem Chabang industrial estate, Thailand
Financial services	Development of offshore financial services	<50 ha	None	Offshore financial and non-financial services	Export	Lobuon offshore financial Centre, Malaysia
Software and internet	Development of software and Information Technology services	<20 Has	Adjacent to universities, institutes	Software and other Information Technology services	Export	Dubai Internet City, United Arab Emirates
Airport-based	Air cargo trade and transshipment	<20 ha	Airports	Warehousing, transshipment	Re-export and domestic	Kuala Lumpur airport free zone, Malaysia
Tourism	Integrated tourism development	200–1000 ha	Tourism areas	Resort and other tourism	Domestic and export	Baru Island, Colombia
Logistic parks or cargo villages	Support logistics	< 50 Ha	Airports, ports, transport hubs	Warehousing, transshipment	Re-export	D1 Logistic Park, Czech Republic

2.3 Models of Governance

Models of governance refers to the various systems and structures that are used to control and manage a society or organisation.

In the policy networks approach, governments engage private actors to address complex public interest challenges. Multiple actors, including both public and private entities, collaborate in policy networks to enforce public policies or, in the analysed example, to introduce projects or programs aimed at achieving economic and political goals. The distinctiveness lies in the intricate interplay between numerous actors who possess diverse strategies and aims. Policy networks, according to definitions by specific authors (Kenis & Schneider, 1991), remain stable networks of ties between actors that pool together resources to effectively implement shared policies. This definition encompasses all individuals involved in the development and implementation of public policies (Borzel, 1997). These entities are distinguished by the existence of both official and informal connections between public and private individuals or organisations that have common interests and goals (Galey & Youngs, 2014).

Researchers frequently apply the policy network approach to examine and evaluate policy-making processes (Dowding, 1995; Moberg, 2014), as well as to ascertain the governance structure of the network (Vollenberg et al., 2007). Additional research has examined the correlation between public management and policy networks (Borzel, 1997) or investigated the connection between privatisation and corporate governance (Martinez et al., 2013).

The decision to adopt the policy network approach as a fundamental tool for comprehension is driven by the intricate nature of the subject under investigation, which includes a complex network of connections among government agencies, private industries, and local and international investors concurrently. The SEZ is a network where different public and private entities formally and informally collaborate to carry out an economic development initiative.

The argument highlights that it establishes the structure for evaluating the intricate network management system, devising strategies, and demonstrating the environment in which institutional interactions between organisations evolve (Klijn & Koppenjan, 2000).

Many studies examining Special Economic Zones (SEZs) have primarily examined economic factors, with only a few exploring governance models, network management policies, or utilising the policy network approach as an alternative means to improve the efficiency of these special zones (Borzel, 1997; Galey & Youngs, 2014).

The presence of a dedicated governance system is a key characteristic that enables us to classify a designated portion of territory, intended for manufacturing or service activities, or for managing activities under a more favourable regime compared to the 'ordinary' one, as a special economic zone. We accomplish this by establishing an organisation, or multiple organisations with varying responsibilities, levels of independence, and operational capability, capable of effectively managing the 'special' system and guaranteeing the full utilisation of its specific provisions by both current and potential investors (Farole, 2011). An effective and stable institutional framework is crucial for the development of any Special Economic Zone (SEZ). Investors consider other aspects beyond just high-quality infrastructure, access to labour, low-cost input elements, or attractive economic-financial incentives when choosing a certain location. Generally, the regulatory scope and governance model must align with the specific attributes of the SEZ proposal and the institutional framework of the host country. The country's political, bureaucratic, and social environment, as well as the Special Economic Zones (SEZ) governance model and its effectiveness, significantly contribute to attracting investments and maintaining a competitive edge over time. These factors are essential for achieving the anticipated development objectives established during the establishment of the SEZ. It is important to highlight that in certain instances, the regulatory and governance experimentation implemented in Special Economic Zones (SEZ) has served as a significant testing ground for the host country to introduce changes to national regulations and apply successful practices from SEZ to other situations (Chen, 2019).

The governance models of Special Economic Zones (SEZs) differ depending on the characteristics and goals of the zones, the political system of the country, and the level of centralisation or decentralisation in terms of the delegations and responsibilities assigned to public entities governing different territories. Administrative divisions such as regions or provinces in the Italian system exemplify this. Additionally, the involvement of private actors in the strategic and operational management of individual zones also plays a role.

The institutional architecture of the Special Economic Zones (SEZ) is intricate, as it encompasses a diverse range of entities, both public and private, each with distinct responsibilities. The political and economic circumstances of numerous nations significantly influence it. Special economic zones do not adhere to a single governance model; however, many shared characteristics can be identified across all sorts of arrangements. While the Special Economic Zones (SEZ) share similarities with regard to their structure and the key actors engaged (government, authorities, promoters, operators, and users), they differ in terms of governance, specifically in terms of the legal status, functions, and obligations of the individuals involved.

When considering their qualities, we can recognise three distinct governance models (Chen, 2019).

2.3.1 Public Management

In the public model, public institutions are responsible for managing activities and areas at both the national and local levels. The governments exercise direct control over the activities in the zones, sometimes assigning development tasks and oversight responsibilities to agencies or partially or totally state-owned corporations. The main governing body is responsible for supervising and coordinating all activities in the SEZ. For instance, this is true for free zones in Iran and certain African regions (such as Zambia, Kenya, Botswana, and Nigeria), as well as many Asian countries (including Iran, Jordan, Pakistan, Bangladesh, and Vietnam), where governmental administration commonly oversees the governance of these zones. Most initiatives fall under the responsibility of government oversight. Efficient assistance and financial resources are necessary for the running and growth of the areas. Additional noteworthy achievements encompass the operational regions in China, Singapore, and Malaysia, which more accurately exemplify the influence of governmental entities or state-owned firms on the effectiveness of Special Economic Zone (SEZ) initiatives (Farole & Moberg, 2014).

2.3.2 *Private Management*

The World Bank's study on Special Economic Zones (Buba & Wong, 2017) demonstrates the recent surge in the number of zones under private management. One reason for this is that other stakeholders play a crucial role in supplying the primary resources, thereby reducing the burden on the public actor. Typically, the central government is responsible for setting the rules and granting licences to private individuals or organisations to commence their operations. Private actors involved in fostering development possess significant operational independence and are accountable to the SEZ authorities, who have limited and well-defined regulatory authority. Private entities have the authority to make independent decisions regarding their long-term management and policy development. They are also responsible for granting access to individuals with whom they establish investment agreements and oversee property lease arrangements, among other things. Local firms form a network around the private actor. This network facilitates the dissemination and transfer of knowledge. Georgia, Serbia, the Philippines, Indonesia, India, and Uruguay are examples of regions under private management.

2.3.3 *Hybrid Forms*

The hybrid model can be regarded as a fusion of the two preceding types. Public and private entities often collaborate to establish a joint organisation referred to as a public–private partnership (PPP). In such instances, the founding country will possess the authority to regulate and oversee the special zone, with the government actively engaging in its establishment and operation to promote private sector engagement in the project (OCSE, 2017). The defining feature of this form is the actors' autonomy in formulating strategic plans, developing operational programs, and establishing working techniques. In general, the public actor is responsible for developing a regulatory framework that is transparent and unambiguous, providing efficient services, managing the finance of essential infrastructure, and supervising private developers or operators.

This model provides policymakers with significant freedom to customise the special economic zones' regimes according to the activities of the area and specific investment projects. Moreover, it facilitates the increased participation of local authorities. For instance, they can assume sole responsibility for the development and promotion of the area. This hybrid technique is prevalent in Ethiopia, Poland, the United Arab Emirates, Panama, Costa Rica, Colombia, Indonesia, Egypt, Mexico, and India.

2.4 Case Studies

2.4.1 Iran

Iran has around 30 designated special economic zones spread across approximately 14 provinces. Out of all these, Tehran possesses the greatest quantity of special zones. The State directs the management of each special zone through a government-formed authority. According to Iranian laws, the Supreme Council of Free Trade and Special Economic Zones must recommend the creation of a new Special Economic Zone (SEZ), and the Cabinet and Parliament must then approve it. The Council of Ministers is responsible for determining or modifying the organisation in charge of the new Special Economic Zone (SEZ). When discussing the operating zones in Iran, it is crucial to highlight that most of them are designated as free trade zones (FTZ). These zones have specific customs procedures and offer advantages for all types of economic enterprises. Iran established its inaugural free trade zone in the late 1970s (Kish Island) (Table 2.5).

The management oversees each sector via a Board of Directors, which includes three to five individuals appointed by the Council of Ministers. Iran's zones follow the distinct regulations outlined in 'The Law on the Establishment and Administration of Economic Zones in the Islamic Republic of Iran'. This legislation comprises 25 articles and 12 notes, encompassing every aspect related to operations, management, and governance within the specified areas. Although Iran has a comprehensive regulation governing the SEZ and FTZ areas, various actors, including agencies and organisations operating in these special zones, are starting to independently implement their own regulations and management plans for the zones, instead of adhering to a unified strategy. We can attribute this to a lack of coordination and network strategies among state agencies, as well as an inadequate focus on coordinated management in the relevant domains.

Table 2.5 Free trade zones in Iran. *Source*: our elaboration

Free trade zone	Establishment year	Area	Location	Authority	Projects
Anzali Port	2003	9400 ha	Caspian Sea/North of Iran	Ports and shipping organisation	• Tourism industry • Agriculture and fishery
Chabahar Free Trade–Industrial Zone (CFZ)	1992	140 ha	Southeast	Chabahar free zone organisation	• Energy hub • Food and tourism industry • Products rooted in the sea-based economy • ITC services
Kish	1989	91.5 km^2	Persian gulf	Kish free zone organisation	• Tourism industry • Banking and financial services • Electronic industries • Marine drilling technology
Arvand	2004	37,400 ha	Northwest of Persian gulf	Arvand free zone organisation	• Heavy and marine installation • Oil and petrochemical industries
Qeshm Free Trade Industrial Zone	1990	480 km^2	Persian gulf and the sea of Oman	Qeshm free zone organisation	• Fishery industries and industrial fishing • Energy Park • Oil logistics services • Transit and transportation industry
ARAS	2005	9700 ha	Northwest of Iran	Jolfa development company	• Transportation and transit industries • Expansion of agricultural, animal husbandry, and transformational industries
MAKOU	2010	5000 ha	Northwest of Iran	Maku free zone is governed by an independent legal entity, and its capital completely belongs to the government.	• Large agricultural and industrial units • Transportation and transit of goods

2.4.2 The United Arab Emirates

The United Arab Emirates has over 40 operational free zones that entice investors and promote foreign investments by streamlining the processes involved in setting up new enterprises. Its primary focus revolves around free trade zones (ports and airports) (Table 2.6). Dubai is a remarkable example of success, with more than 20 free trade zones that contribute to its impressive export capabilities and the significant sum of money spent.

Private companies or public–private partnerships typically operate in most special zones. Additionally, an independent authority governs each specific zone, controlling the appropriate licensing and project management.

The UAE has built special zones for financial services, information technology, and scientific businesses. Several countries in the Middle East have implemented the United Arab Emirates' concept for managing special zones. An instance of this can be seen in the Astana International Financial Centre (AIFC) in Kazakhstan, which was founded following the Dubai model.

The governance of the Special Economic Zones in the United Arab Emirates is intricate. Despite the existence of a comprehensive regulatory framework that applies to all areas, each zone has its own unique set of legislation.

Each region in the UAE has its own Free Zone Authority (FZA), which oversees the governance of special zones and adheres to the compulsory trade laws set by the federal government. In order to develop the system, the UAE governments have augmented their investments by diversifying them into industries beyond oil operations. In order to attract more investors and streamline corporate operations, the UAE government has built numerous centres. Establishing cluster-based specialised economic zones is another way to attract attention.

In the United Arab Emirates, the government's economic development strategy prioritises private developments over public ones. Private and foreign actors have primarily been involved in the main projects, with a special focus on the ICT and technology sectors. As a result, there is a need for systems to coordinate and communicate in order to manage the connections between the government and investors, with the goal of establishing and enhancing efficient networks.

The United Arab Emirates is investing significantly in technology to enhance connectivity among network actors and free zones, which include the government, state agencies, and private sectors. The DMCC free zone serves as an illustration of this, employing electronic signatures to oversee legal services, while the Business Apps Manager ensures adherence to the United Arab Emirates' regulations.

Table 2.6 Free zones in UAE—some cases. *Source*: our elaboration

	Year of establishment	Area	Ownership				Authority
Jebel Ali Free Zone	1985	57 km^2	Free Zone Company (FZCO), multiple	Shareholding	Free Zone Establishment (FZE)	Branch of a foreign or UAE company	Jebel Ali Free Zone
Masdar City	2009	6 km^2	Free zone limited liability company (FZ-LLC)	Branch of a foreign or UAE company			Abu Dhabi future energy company
Dubai airport free zone (DAFZ)	1996	69 km^2	Free zone limited liability company (FZ-LLC)	Branch of a foreign or UAE company			Authorised by Dubai airport free zone (DAFZ)
Dubai multi-commodities Centre (DMCC)	2002	200-ha	Free zone limited liability company (FZ-LLC)	Branch of a foreign or UAE company			Established by government and Ahmed bin Sulayem is the executive chairman of DMCC. Authorised by Dubai multi-commodities Centre (DMCC)
Dubai international financial Centre (DIFC)	2004	110 ha	Company limited by shares	Branch of a foreign or UAE company			Independent authority by Dubai international financial Centre, FC has its own independent, internationally regulated regulator and judicial system

References

Akinci, G., & Crittle, J. (2008). *Special economic zone: Performance, lessons learned, and implication for zone development* (Vol. No. 45869, pp. 1–83). The World Bank.

Berni, A., & Moschera, L. (2021). La letteratura su policy network e modelli di governance. In AA. VV (Ed.), *R. Realfonzo, Le politiche per lo sviluppo in Campania ZES, piano del lavoro, aree di crisi* (pp. 43–58). UNIOR Press. ISBN: 978-88-6719-201-4.

Borzel, T. A. (1997). *Organizing Babylon: on the different conceptions of policy networks*. Public Administration.

Buba, J., & Wong, M. D. (2017). *Special economic zones: an operational review of their impacts*.

Chen, X. (2019). *Change and continuity in special economic zones: a reassessment and lessons from China*.

Dowding, K. (1995). Model or metaphor? A critical review of the policy network approach. *Political Studies, 43*(1), 136–158.

Farole, T. (2011). Special Economic Zones in Africa. Comparing Performance and Learning from Global Experiences. Directions in Development—Trade, n. 60059—The World Bank, Washington.

Farole, T., & Moberg, L. (2014). *It worked in China, so why not in Africa? The political economy challenge of Special Economic Zones (No. 2014/152)*. WIDER Working Paper.

Galey, S., & Youngs, P. (2014). *Moving towards an Integrated Theory of Policy Networks: A Multi-Theoretical Approach for Examining State-Level Policy Change in US Subsystems*. Working Paper# 45. Education Policy Center at Michigan State University.

Kenis, P. N., & Schneider, V. (1991). Policy networks and policy analysis: Scrutinizing a new analytical toolbox. In B. Marin & R. Mayntz (Eds.), *Policy networks: Empirical evidence and theoretical considerations* (pp. 25–59). Westview Press.

Klijn, E. H., & Koppenjan, J. F. (2000). Public management and policy networks: Foundations of a network approach to governance. *Public Management an International Journal of Research and Theory, 2*(2), 135–158.

Martinez, M., Jamison, M., & Tillmar, M. (2013). Public utilities corporate governance. *Journal of Management & Governance, 17*(4), 827–833.

Maryami, S., Pezzillo, I. M., Martinez, M., & Berni, A. (2019). Special economic zones' governance and organizational structures: Comparative study by focusing on a policy network approach in Iran, UAE and Kazakhstan. In *Knowledge ecosystems and growth: 14th international forum on knowledge asset dynamics - IFKAD 2019*. IKAM—Institute of Knowledge Assets Management.

Moberg, L. (2014). *The political economy of special economic zones*. Forthcoming in the Journal of Institutional Economics, SSRN.2297871.

OCSE. (2017). *Criticises European plan to tax internet giants*. Telecom 14 September 2017.

Sun, Y., & Cao, C. (2018). The evolving relations between government agencies of innovation policymaking in emerging economies: A policy network approach and its application to the Chinese case. *Research Policy, 47*(3), 592–605.

Unido. (2015). *Economic zones in the Asean industrial parks, special economic zones, eco industrial parks, innovation districts as strategies for industrial competitiveness*. Unido - United Nations Industrial Development Organization - Country Office in Vietnam.

United Nations Conference on Trade and Development. (2019). *World investment report 2019: Special economic zones*. UN.

Vats, A., DeClerq, M., Clements, S., & Chen, X. (2018). *Special Economic Zones as a Tool for Economic Development*.

Vollenberg, M., Kenis, P., & Raab, J. (2007, October). Provan and Milward 1995 revisited: A case-study on network structure and network effectiveness of a Dutch mental health care network. In *9th Public Management Research Conference, Tucson, Arizona October*.

Chapter 3
Special Economic Zones Worldwide: Governance Models and Regulations for Work

3.1 Introduction

The chapter aims to evaluate the current state of Special Economic Zones Governance models, regulatory frameworks, special economic zones, and case studies (SEZs), beginning with their objectives and global distribution and subsequently examining the primary governance models.[1] The goal of the contribution is to pinpoint, through the analysis of several international cases of special zone activation, beneficial policies and interventions that can be considered when designing governance and formulating specific labour policies for the settlement of a new SEZ. Regardless of their success or failure, we consider the most pertinent special zone cases, as well as the consistent characteristics and objectives among the analysed countries and the regions that the SEZ will focus on.

The review is useful for both accessing the best and worst practice models and identifying potential issues that may arise because of past experiences. In recent years, there has been a growing emphasis among scholars and researchers on the development of special economic zones (SEZs) as a valuable instrument for promoting economic growth, stimulating employment, and boosting investments through tax incentives and economic benefits. International experience indicates that the establishment of innovation, the enhancement of development, and competitiveness are contingent upon the relationships between various institutional actors, including national and local governments, agencies, and public and private organisations. On the one hand, many studies focus on the SEZ's economic impact. On the other hand, a smaller number of studies tend to investigate the impact of other characteristics (such as management, governance, actors' roles, and the institutional framework) on the success of these special areas. Therefore, it is fascinating

[1] This paragraph contains a summary of various research studies published on the topic (Ciociano et al. 2020a, b).

A. Berni, *The Complex Environments of Special Economic Zones*,
SpringerBriefs in Economics, https://doi.org/10.1007/978-3-031-83425-7_3

to explore the governance mechanism and the role of the actors within the network from its inception.

The presence of a dedicated governance system is a critical characteristic that enables us to designate a portion of territory as a special economic zone, irrespective of its specific classification. To ensure that both actual and potential investors can completely benefit from the specific provisions of the 'special' regime, we establish an entity (or multiple entities) with varying roles, levels of autonomy, and operational capacity. This allows us to efficiently manage the regime (Farole, 2011). Therefore, the creation of an effective and efficient institutional framework is one of the most critical success factors in any special economic zone. In order to set up themselves in a specific region, numerous investors do not necessitate high-quality infrastructure, access to labour, low-cost input factors, or more or less enticing economic or financial incentives.

Many countries that have established Special Economic Zones without a general governance model or institutional framework to increase their appeal have failed to consider the fact that the political, bureaucratic, and social context, as well as the governance model used for the SEZs and its effectiveness, are critical factors in attracting investments and maintaining a competitive edge over time. Therefore, these nations have failed to achieve the development objectives set at the time of the establishment of the Special Economic Zones. Nevertheless, in specific instances, SEZs have functioned as a significant 'laboratory' for the host nation, generating new momentum for the modification of national regulations and the extension of effectively tested best practices to other institutional and bureaucratic contexts (Vats et al., 2018). The governance models of Special Economic Zones are characterised by a variety of factors, including the political system of the country, the degree of centralisation/decentralisation at the territorial level (in terms of delegations and responsibilities for direction and management assigned to public entities responsible for governing more or less extensive areas of territory; for example, in an administrative division logic reminiscent of the Italian system, regions or provinces), the greater or lesser role of private entities in the strategic and operational management of individual areas, and other supplementary factors.

3.2 Special Economic Zones Around the World

We have examined labour market policies implemented in the Special Economic Zones (SEZs), as well as the governance methods applied within. We have organised them geographically to facilitate the comparison of macroeconomic scenarios and the distinct features of the locations when the intervention occurred.

For each area, it is possible to list the strengths of recent or past experiences relevant to the design solutions for emerging SEZs, along with the challenges that have been encountered that could lead to the implementation of preventative measures.

3.2.1 Africa

Most African nations established Special Economic Zones (SEZs) in the 1990s and 2000s. However, countries such as Senegal and Liberia established Free Trade Zones (FTZs) in the 1970s. For example, the Arab Republic of Egypt, the Syrian Arab Republic, Israel, and Jordan established government-administered zones in the 1960s and 1970s, which overlapped with the initial construction of such zones in the Philippines, the Dominican Republic, the Republic of Korea, and Taiwan. (China). Free trade zones are implemented in many areas of the Middle East and North Africa (Akinci & Crittle, 2008).

Presently, 38 of the 54 nations on the continent accommodate around 273 Special Economic Zones (SEZs) across Africa, including those in the process of formation. United Nations Conference on Trade and Development, 2019. The government, typically an EPZ entity, establishes and supervises most regions, except for Ghana and Kenya. Other nations—Madagascar, Mali, Mauritius, and the Seychelles—have established unique EPZ manufacturing programs that have minimally influenced employment growth and exports. China has played a pivotal role in economic and commercial partnerships in the creation of African Special Economic Zones, acting as the principal foreign partner and investor, especially in Egypt, Zambia, Ethiopia, Mauritius, Algeria, Angola, Kenya, and Nigeria. Chinese firms, supported by the Ministry of Economy and local government, have facilitated the creation of Special Economic Zones (SEZs) in these cases. The partnership to establish Special Economic Zones (SEZs) has facilitated the creation of industrial parks, as seen in Egypt and Ethiopia. The SEZ, predominantly financed by Chinese investment, functions as a crucial platform for China's involvement strategy in Africa, highlighting mutual benefits for the involved parties. Thus, it is identifiable as a unique and innovative model of growth and cooperation for Africa, significantly impacting both local and Chinese labour forces (Brautigam & Xiaoyang, 2011). The investments are varied; generally, those associated with agricultural operations that utilise natural resources or traditional activities of the host region predominate. The primary industries in African regions encompass clothes, textiles, and food (Akinci & Crittle, 2008). The Special Economic Zones predominantly necessitate labour in the textile and apparel sector (90% in Mauritius and Madagascar, 33% in Kenya, 11% in Tanzania and Zimbabwe), agricultural operations (60% in Ghana, 50% in Zimbabwe, 18% in Kenya), and supplementary activities related to services and light industry (Kingombe & te Velde, 2013).

The Tangier Free Zone in Morocco is significant, consisting of two centres: Tangier-Med and the Tangier Free Zone (TFZ), located 14 km from Spain and ideally placed on the transit route between Africa, Europe, Asia, North America, and South America. The city's strategic location has transformed it into a logistical hub for several European ports, reliant on just-in-time production methodologies. This mostly operates within the agri-food, textile and leather, mechanical, electronic, chemical, metallurgical, and high-technology sectors. It spans 500 hectares and is scheduled to endure for a decade. The OECD forecasts the creation of 47,000 employment over 10 years, emphasising a substantial supply of affordable skilled labour (Böhmer, 2011).

For analytical purposes, the most compelling aspects of the African experience pertain to socioeconomic characteristics that are also observable in the labour market of some italian regions, albeit with varying degrees and manifestations. Informal work and unemployment primarily impact youngsters and women. In sub-Saharan Africa, non-agricultural employment within the informal economy accounts for 66% of total employment, whereas in North Africa, it comprises 52%. In 2014, the estimated proportion of vulnerable workers was 76.6% (ILO, 2015). Some employment initiatives aim to enhance women's integration into the labour market and achieve wage equality. The imperative of adequately training the workforce to meet the demand for skilled labour is another factor to consider.

Regarding the implemented procedures in the African Special Economic Zones, the use of fixed-term contracts is widespread. Temporary employment is beneficial for foreign management to sustain a flexible workforce. Other common techniques include long-term permits for foreign workers (long-term visas), as demonstrated by Senegal, and more flexible hiring and termination restrictions, as seen in Ivory Coast. Standard approaches have included the implementation of targeted tax incentives for employment and the establishment of regulations or agreements to ensure labour market stability. The circumstances in South Africa and Nigeria exemplify effective models, guaranteeing the elimination of strikes or blockades in all 17 Special Economic Zones within the region (Newman & Page, 2017).

Regarding the achieved results, despite the widespread establishment of special economic zones around the continent intended to promote growth, the success of these projects has fallen short of expectations due to many issues.

The essential qualities comprise inadequate institutional resources, restricted political and administrative capabilities, and the absence or inadequacy of monitoring and evaluation procedures (Kingombe & te Velde, 2013; Woolfrey, 2013). In 2006, the ILO gathered data indicating that the impact of Special Economic Zones (SEZs) on diminishing unemployment is minimal in both the public and private sectors, with notable outliers in Lesotho, Nigeria, Madagascar, and Kenya (Kingombe & te Velde, 2013). The remuneration and perks afforded to employees in Special Economic Zones (SEZs) frequently match those recognised for comparable positions outside these zones, including within the African setting (Woolfrey, 2013).

The empirical assessments of the status of existing SEZ projects in several sub-Saharan African countries produce disappointing outcomes. The African engagement with Special Economic Zones (SEZs) has been predominantly disappointing, lacking the necessary physical, institutional, and human infrastructure to entice global investors (Newman & Page, 2017). The impact on employment is negligible, and the connections between Special Economic Zones (SEZs) and the adjacent local economy are typically weak, with entrepreneurial density far lower than the average business density found in SEZs throughout Asia or Latin America.

Given these factors, it is important to highlight many significant issues. A comprehensive overhaul of work culture and social policy is necessary, as they insufficiently protect fundamental rights. The persistent divergence from ILO standards endures, and the limited union membership among workers is due to prohibitive legislation. Until 2005, Kenya prohibited employees in the EPZ from participating in unions or collective bargaining (Farole, 2011). The persistent reliance on temporary labour may arise from rigid labour markets, and Special Economic Zones (SEZs) can negatively impact social circumstances and employment quality, particularly disadvantaging women who are under-represented in managerial or supervisory positions. Observations reveal a significant reliance on foreign labour rather than developing and employing the local workforce. Investors in several African nations face challenges in finding necessary technological competence and adequately qualified workers. Many organisations must substantially engage in training, often by temporarily moving local personnel for educational purposes. This regulation may impose a considerable financial strain on investors. Few effective instances exist of training institutes collaborating with colleges and universities to cultivate a trained workforce (Zeng, 2016). In addition to the unique characteristics of each nation, essential factors influencing the effectiveness of Special Economic Zones (SEZs) encompass institutional efficacy, the fight against and prevention of corruption, and deficiencies in planning, management, and oversight of executed projects, which are often hindered by political and administrative instability (Kingombe & te Velde, 2013; Woolfrey, 2013). The failure whether total or partial of the labour and industrial policies enacted in the Special Economic Zones (SEZ) is due to inadequate institutional coordination and ineffective industrialisation strategies, frequently exacerbated by a chronic shortage of raw materials and insufficient infrastructure, encompassing electrical services, transportation, and water supplies. This situation highlights the direct relationship between the administration and strategic capacities of the host country and the performance results attainable in different sectors, including labour, through the creation of Special Economic Zones (SEZs). Regarding the administration of states with Special Economic Zones (SEZs), it is significant that, according to the World Bank's 2017 administration Indicators surveys, Africa remains inferior to Asia in 'Regulatory Quality'. This concerns a government's ability to create and enforce regulations and laws that promote the growth of the private sector.

Specifically, Botswana and South Africa are situated on a percentile nearly resembling the average of the lowest performing European countries, including Italy, and at times even surpass it. In the late 1980s, influenced by international financiers, particularly the World Bank, the concept arose in Africa that private sector development was crucial for wealth generation. African institutions and the ruling class embraced these principles in the 1990s. In 2002, the NEPAD (New Partnership for Africa's Development) declared that improving market efficiency was crucial for alleviating poverty and achieving sustainable development, hence promoting private direct investments. Many African states have embraced this new paradigm, which includes the creation of Special Economic Zones (SEZs) across different countries, despite the persistent acknowledgement of a substantial disparity between policy development and its actual execution (Cajati & Gattamorta, 2010).

The reasons are varied, primarily due to the numerous and distinct underlying conditions that foster a robust market and entrepreneurial growth. The World

Table 3.1 SEZ in Africa—summary

SEZ in Africa. Strengths and weaknesses	
Botswana	– Enhancement of production chains – Internationalisation of training – Strengthening of the education and vocational training system – Involvement and collaboration with private entities and institutions
Ethiopia	– Public–private partnership model in the National Technical and vocational education and training (TVET) system – Highly specialised training institute (Ethiopian textile industry development institute—ETIDI) – Facilitated visa procedures for qualified expatriate managers to train non-emigrant Ethiopians – Accusations against foreign companies for hiring compatriots to the detriment of locals in key positions – Low productivity due to the transition from rural to urban environment (due to the low qualification of workers) – Extreme working conditions
Egypt	– Housing allocation programs and child subsidies for children of workers active in the SEZ – Layoffs regulated by less strict rules than outside the SEZ (if caused by low productivity and/or worker qualifications)
South Africa	– Tax breaks and incentives related to employment relationships (Employment Tax Incentive Act, 2013)
Nigeria	– Office of labour and employment services for each area – Special permissions for foreign workers in the SEZ

Economic Forum delineates the impediments to entrepreneurial vigour and private sector advancement in Africa in the following order: access to financing; inefficient governmental bureaucracy; restrictive labour regulations; subpar work ethic among the national workforce; inflation; tax regulations; insufficient infrastructure; tax burden; financial regulations concerning foreign currency; low educational attainment of the workforce; corruption; inadequate public health; political instability; and crime.

In specific cases, the establishment and regulation of SEZs have sought to successfully remove certain obstacles to development (Table 3.1).

3.2.2 *Middle East*

The SEZs in the Middle East are not comparable to the more historically significant regions of Latin America or Asia, particularly due to a longstanding preference for commercial over-productive activity. Jordan, Iran, and the Jebel Ali Free Zone in Dubai—a government-established regional distribution and logistics centre—are notable outliers. Dubai has taken a prominent role in establishing special zones, such as Internet City and Media City, which facilitate the export of IT and multimedia services. Abu Dhabi is constructing a $3.3 billion offshore financial services zone and a commodities market on Saadiyat Island (Akinci & Crittle, 2008).

The experience in Jordan is the most relevant, especially for programs aimed at increasing female participation in the workforce. Development policies prioritise the empowerment of women in developing or transitioning economies, not only to achieve gender equality in wages and employment but also to enhance their role in society and the domestic environment. In family management, women play a crucial role in managing the household's finances and uplifting the family community from poverty, often becoming the primary source of income.

The gender equality objectives for the Italian labour market primarily focus on increasing women's employment and achieving wage parity. An additional aspect to include in the SEZs employment actions could be the evaluation of policies for reconciling family care times with work and, more generally, incentives for hiring women, who are particularly vulnerable workers in the South of Italy.

The legislator should concentrate on managing foreign workers, particularly highly qualified individuals, as previously discussed. Dubai is another example of this, having resorted to limiting entry quotas precisely to avoid the displacement effect of foreign workers on local ones. From the Iranian experience, we must consider the legislative differences between SEZ and the rest of the country. In the SEZ, excessive labour market flexibility can negatively impact a workforce whose rights are already inadequately, if not completely, protected within the SEZ establishment. Furthermore, the extensive and mandatory use of digital payments is a crucial factor in addressing the informal nature of labour relations because it ensures the traceability of payments and the reasons behind their movements (Table 3.2).

Table 3.2 SEZ in the Middle East—summary

SEZ in the Middle East. Strengths and weaknesses	
Iran	– *Regulations of Employment of Human Resources, Insurance and Social Security in the Free Trade—Industrial Zone,* more flexible and less detailed than Iran's Labour Code, more restrictive and specific – Workers' rights poorly protected – Scant regulations on occupational safety and health
Jordan	– Ad hoc measures for women from rural areas employed in SEZs – Satellite factory program, aimed at rural women to provide them access to job opportunities near their villages – The spread of digital payments for wages, also included as an option in collective bargaining, serves to ensure transparency and certainty of payments
Dubai	– Maximum quotas for immigrant employment in the private sector, especially for administrative jobs – Priority for national workers has a right of priority on the possibility of employment – There are no unions; strikes or production stoppages are prohibited

3.2.3 *Asia*

The performance of Special Economic Zones (SEZs) in Asia has been notable, particularly in China and India.

Special economic zones have enhanced the quality of the current workforce via training initiatives and skills enhancement through the formalisation of employment arrangements (the ILO estimates that 68.2% of workers in Asia and the Pacific are informal). The Chinese government has built training institutes to enhance the technical and professional competencies of workers. In Taiwan, collaborative training programs among schools, colleges, and enterprises within special economic zones have effectively cultivated capabilities. In the Philippines, there has been a notable enhancement in skill levels, emphasising research endeavours and elevating professionalism (Akinci & Crittle, 2008). In nations such as Thailand, enterprises experiencing a persistent shortage of trained personnel are instituting initiatives to create human resource development centres within their industrial facilities. The establishment of private special zones is a contemporary trend in Asia, especially in Southeast Asian countries such as Indonesia, Thailand, and the Philippines (Akinci & Crittle, 2008). In recent years, the Export Processing Zones (EPZs) within the Special Economic Zones have gained increased attention due to their ability to facilitate the influx of foreign investments, particularly in labour-intensive industries (Remedio, 1996). The special economic zones in the Philippines have a distinct function. A limited number of areas have witnessed a concentration of new employment opportunities. The SEZ's capacity to provide new employment opportunities may draw workers from other regions, perhaps resulting in migratory flows that, due to increased labour supply, may not mitigate the unemployment issue. Consequently, Special Economic Zones exert a dual impact on employment, predominantly fostering the creation of new jobs in Asian countries. The nations with the greatest quantity of designated special regions are China, the Philippines, and India.

The analysis of the Asian setting is pertinent to the enhancement of skills and workforce specialisations, which are intrinsically associated with vocational and on-the-job training. Despite recurring challenges in regulating job agreements concerning hours, health and safety, and social security protections, the employment contracts formed in the SEZ are typically more consistent than those in the remainder of the country. Nonetheless, the issue of irregular work arrangements persists as a significant concern. Thus, we can use the designated area as a strategy to combat the underground economy.

3.2.3.1 China

China is a pivotal backdrop in the global landscape for the establishment and results of SEZs. Shenzhen, the preeminent one, has implemented substantial structural reforms, encompassing a novel labour contract structure, an overhauled residency permit framework tailored for migrant workers, and an updated salary system, all of which have facilitated its success. Indeed, 80% of the engaged labour force comprises migrants, particularly young adults aged 16–25 years (Wang, 2013; Wei, 1999). Over 67% of the current workforce has attained secondary education, in contrast to 49% of the preceding generation; they exhibit digital literacy and are predominantly unmarried. The Shenzhen Special Economic Zone has experienced a metamorphosis in its GDP composition, transitioning from dominance in the agricultural sector to significant expansion in the secondary and tertiary sectors. The expansion of the secondary sector (from 20.5% in 1978 to 50.1% in 2007) and the tertiary sector (from 42.5% in 1978 to 49.8% in 2007) has counterbalanced the reduction in agriculture (from 37% in 1978 to 4.1% in 1990 and 0.1% in 2007). The primary sectors of development are four: high-tech industry, logistics, finance, and culture (including tourism, entertainment, educational resources, and mass media). The establishment of this Special Economic Zone has heavily relied on the recruitment of female workers from rural regions (Ngai, 2004). Shenzhen serves as a centre for innovative manufacturing, particularly in electronic products. In 1998, high tech enterprises constituted at least 40% of the industrial production in the Special Economic Zone, representing about one-third of Guangdong province's industrial profits (Leong & Pratap, 2011). Notwithstanding the escalating cost of living, China's technological advancement has not resulted in a parallel improvement in working circumstances or an augmentation of pay. China receives a poor ranking in the World Bank's evaluation of overall governance (World Bank, Worldwide Governance Indicators, 2018), particularly regarding the degree of democratic involvement. The establishment of Chinese Special Economic Zones began in 1978 as a potential model for development and investment attractiveness, coinciding with the launch of economic reforms to rectify the shortcomings of Maoist economic policy. The initiation of a project in Guangdong in 1979 established the foundation for the creation of the inaugural Chinese Special Economic Zones in 1984. This was predicated on multiple regulatory measures from the State Council, one for each sector, alongside a suite of legislation designed to govern trade transactions, the establishment of foreign firms within Chinese territory, and other aspects, in a manner that was distinct and more market oriented. In the initial phase, the State Council specifically prioritised investments from overseas enterprises with Chinese money as well as those from Hong Kong and Macao, emphasising high-tech industries. Both the incentive structure and the significant autonomy granted to the regions and their governing authorities contribute to the rapid growth of Chinese Special Economic Zones. They possess such autonomy that the statutes regard them equivalently to the provinces (Yuan et al., 2009). Initially, people viewed them as quasi-territorial zones that were independent of the national framework. A tangible barrier initially separated the first special economic zone, Shenzhen, from its surrounding territory, a concept known as the second frontier. Thereafter, it progressively extended to include the entire sub-province, and the removal of mobility restrictions for Chinese residents and enterprises coincided with China's incremental economic and political liberalisation. The sub-provincial city operates as a legislative enclave, enabling the local government to enforce regulatory measures within the framework of national laws. In some cases, the national level has upheld the decisions rendered by the SEZ. From a governance standpoint, these regions demonstrate significant centralisation in sub-provincial administration, as exemplified by the municipality of Shenzhen, which depends on various specialised entities for assistance and oversight of the economic activities conducted within the Special Economic Zone (SEZ). The regulations that govern the utilisation and administration of the various zones vary, with some sections entirely allocated to private firms and others subject to strict public oversight. Most of the time, the public owns the spaces and leases them in exchange for long-term contractual rental costs. The structural reforms implemented in the Shenzhen Special Economic Zone, including a labour contract system, an updated residency permit mechanism for migrant workers, and a revised wage system, have facilitated the establishment of a framework for flexible labour utilisation and profit maximisation while simultaneously exerting downward pressure on wages. They carried out the wage reform at a time when it was considered controversial. They implemented the Shekou wage model in 1983, reorganising salaries into three components: base pay, occupational pay, and variable allowances. The management authorities of the Special Economic Zones instituted a minimum pay and provided a suite of social measures, hitherto unimplemented in China, to all permanent employees and a substantial number of temporary workers. The enhanced social security for workers has drawn migrants from various regions of China to the Special Economic Zones, with over one million temporary workers having already established themselves in the SEZs by 1989. The adoption of a learning-by-doing approach has been a key principle in the development of the Shenzhen Special Economic Zone, serving as a long-term plan to enhance the temporary and non-structural advantages associated with the Special Economic Zone. The SEZ network connecting foreign enterprises and local financiers has been crucial for this achievement. In 1985, 409 industrial projects were active, over 70% of which involved Chinese collaborations; by a decade later, this number had risen to 1400. The concurrent operation with domestic and international enterprises has been crucial for the dissemination of innovations (Yeung et al., 2009). The Special Economic Zones recognise a degree of statutory homogeneity while permitting considerable freedom in execution. This explains why Shenzhen has its own pension system and unemployment benefits. The Shenzhen Special Economic Zone has initiated the promotion of the Collective Consultation Law, after the Shenzhen Law on Industrial Relations (30 clauses, 2008). Intense resistance from industrialists, especially those in Hong Kong, hindered the implementation in 2011. This pertains mostly to rights and collective bargaining talks. Two notably detrimental policies for workers persist: the retention of the hukou system, adversely affecting migrant workers, and the prohibition of the right to association and collective bargaining for employees. These two factors engender significant rigidities within the industrial relations framework. Notwithstanding changes to the residence permit system, it affords access solely to a restricted array of minimum social security benefits. The enactment of the Labour Contract Law in 2007 markedly elevated the proportion of employees possessing formal contracts. Over 70% of employees possessed formal regular contracts; however, 80% of these contracts were short-term (less than 2 years). The law's lack of regulation regarding casual work has led many firms to establish a structure that employs several temporary workers without formal regularisation or contribution requirements. The irregularity in executing the employment contract or the omission of providing a copy to the employee renders it unfeasible for the employee to substantiate the existence and duration of the working connection in the event of a dispute with the employer (Leong & Pratap, 2011).

Based on our analysis of the differences between municipalities that established a Special Economic Zone earlier and those that did so later, we found that the SEZ implementation program positively influences foreign direct investments by promoting agglomeration economies. This resulted in the establishment of two housing registration systems for population management in 1958. It pertains not only to the registration of an individual's abode but also encompasses all information linked to their public and private domains (Ngai, 2004). Workers have experienced more substantial income rises than the growth in the local cost of living. The impacts are diverse. The subsequently established areas experience a reduction in advantages. The average wage for employees at first-institution SEZ has increased by 8%, while the cost of living has increased by 5%, both of which are higher than the figures observed for second-institution SEZ (Wang, 2013). Following the implementation of the Labour Law Contract, there has been a rise in the number of employees with formal employment and regular contracts. The desire for employment has also risen. This has resulted in a rise in employment prospects, particularly for young and unmarried individuals, who tend to regularly switch professions to enhance their status and perceived remuneration. The ease with which employers can terminate employment drives their high mobility, and it is common for hiring managers to resort to informal agreements when labour demand declines, thereby restricting the use of traditional contracts (Leong & Pratap, 2011). Additionally, it is important to note that numerous enterprises in Shenzhen offer free dorms for migrant workers, which are linked to company-affiliated canteens. This establishes a quasi-militarised regime within the organisation, enabling control over employees' lives outside working hours (about 50% of employees utilise the dormitory service), resulting in significant psychological, physical, and social repercussions (Leong & Pratap, 2011; Ngai, 2004). Significant concerns regrettably, a contributing factor to the competitiveness of the Shenzhen region is the exploitation of migrant workers, who represent some of the most vulnerable segments of the labour force, particularly those originating from rural areas, as their wages constitute 40–55% of those of a typical urban worker. This is one of the factors that prompted the implementation of the new management system for migrant workers' permits, intended to modify the local hukou status, which effectively allows for lower compensation for migrant workers compared to local employees. In 2003, Premier Wen Jiabao recognised that millions of migrant workers were either not receiving their wages punctually or not receiving them at all. From 2004 to 2009, Shenzhen implemented a novel residency permit system for migrant workers, marking the first such attempt in China, partly to tackle employment scarcity; however, it did not enhance working and social conditions. Despite the existence of a formal collective bargaining framework, it remains unexecuted. In infrequent instances where employees participate in agreements, they possess minimal or no bargaining power. Corporate management groups frequently exert influence over unions, resulting in diminished power for the latter. The sole method of articulating opposition to negotiations is via strikes. Unlike the earlier protests, these strikes are more definitive, as evidenced by the years 2007 to 2008 and again in 2009 to 2010, which were marked by frequent roadblocks associated with factory strikes, public demonstrations, and organised marches. Collective bargaining is essential for all stakeholders engaged. This clarifies the reasoning behind the discussions about experimental initiatives aimed at enabling corporate unions to participate in collective consultations with management within the Shenzhen Special Economic Zone and beyond. The standard working hours in the Shenzhen Special Economic Zone are 10 h daily, 6 days a week, contravening Chinese legislation, which mandates 8 h per day for 5 days a week. The workers' consent to increased earnings via overtime (roughly 1.5 times the hourly wage for each additional hour) may lead to the hourly exploitation of workers surpassing established thresholds, resulting in substantiated discrimination against migrant labourers. The Shenzhen Special Economic Zone lacks occupational safety and health protection standards. The health repercussions for employees are extensive, and there is a significant demand for support services among those with permanent contracts. Even within standard employment agreements, services frequently go unrendered. The company denies the worker the right to receive a copy of the contract, as it is customary not to supply one (Leong & Pratap, 2011).

3.2.3.2 SEZ in Asia: Some Considerations

The SEZs offer an opportunity to address the expansion of undeclared employment in Asia, as evidenced in Africa. In several nations, including India and China, it is customary to create a fictitious employment contract without supplying a copy to the employee, thus evading the employer's pay and contribution responsibilities. The ramifications for workers' rights are severe, as the absence of evidence of a formal employment relationship results in the forfeiture of all associated social benefits. Consequently, it is essential to guarantee that the formalisation of the job connection is both incentivised and traceable and not readily evaded. Likewise, vigilance about adherence to labour standards must consistently remain up, in stark contrast to the situation in India, where business inspections are often dissuaded or manipulated, and self-certification is permitted. The aim of regulating foreign labour flows should be to safeguard equitable job possibilities and, most importantly, professional advancement for both nationals and foreigners, particularly when local workers face disadvantages. The efficacy of the Asian Special Economic Zones is attributed to specialist skills and technological utilisation; experiential learning and intra-organisational training are essential elements that have facilitated the development of specific competencies. Italy has previously implemented these two forms of training inside job connections (for example, via interprofessional funds), and the SEZ system can further develop and modify them as needed (Table 3.3).

Table 3.3 SEZ in Asia—summary

SEZ in Asia	Strengths and weaknesses
China	– Management of foreign or non-urban labour – Renewed mechanism for residence permits specific to migrant workers and a new wage system – Learning-by-doing – Flexibility in implementing legislation in the SEZs – Management of foreign or non-urban labour – Limited protection of the rights of unguaranteed workers – Discrimination against migrant workers – Hukou system – Exploitation of migrant workers, especially those from rural areas
India	– Extreme working conditions – Strikes are an illegal activity – Non-existent or superficial labour inspections – Self-certification of compliance with labour regulations

3.2.4 America

The Americas is characterised by the extensive use of zones to promote export development and enhance trade. Free trade zones and export processing zones have expanded significantly during the last 30 years. They possess a lengthy history in Latin America, originating in the early nineteenth century. Since 2010, there have been numerous initiatives aimed at revitalising the Special Economic Zones as drivers of economic growth and employment. The region presently contains over 500 Special Economic Zones that accommodate over 10,000 enterprises and provide employment for around one million individuals. They are present in nearly all economies of Central and South America, excluding Suriname and Guyana.

The experiences in special zones in the Dominican Republic and Costa Rica and private industrial parks in Mexico have resulted in the implementation of a private management model in most instances, despite their initial public management. The Mexican maquiladora exemplifies privatised administration under a governmental initiative (Akinci & Crittle, 2008). Comprehending the effects of Special Economic Zones in Latin America is challenging, as economic incentives have paradoxically led to a rise in illicit activities, with underground economies and black markets linked to SEZs being prevalent (Reyes, 2011). The United States holds the largest number of special zones, followed by the Dominican Republic, Nicaragua, and Colombia, all of which emphasise informality and female employment. In the United States, foreign trade zones, referred to as SEZs, are predominantly free trade zones designed to incentivise enterprises to conduct distribution or production activities domestically instead of outsourcing. The sectors most impacted include oil refining, automobiles, electronics, pharmaceuticals, and manufacturing and equipment.

The Americas host a multitude of special economic zones, especially in Latin America. Once more, the use of the SEZs as an instrument to address informal

Table 3.4 SEZs in America—summary

SEZ in America	Strengths and weaknesses
Panama	– Evidence on the generation of positive spillover effects from immigrants in the labour market of the SEZs
Colombia	– The hiring cost for the company includes contributions to the social security system – Tax incentives for hiring

labour and promote women's participation in the labour market is a subject of study. Panama exemplifies a particular zone that reaps the advantages of spillover effects, a phenomenon wherein production, expertise, and knowledge from a corporation or a more confined area disseminate to adjacent entities without incurring initial expenses. Regulating free-riding behaviours is essential for sustaining competitiveness and fostering research and technical innovation in industrial districts. In Panama, skilled immigration produces spillover effects that enhance the specialisation, productivity, and competencies of the workforce in the SEZs, thereby benefiting local workers as well (Table 3.4).

3.2.5 *Europe and Russia*

Europe hosts around 91 free zones, which encompass special economic zones (SEZs). Founded in 1959, the Shannon Duty-Free Processing Zone in Ireland holds significant importance; Shannon Development, a regional development agency, manages it to attract international investment and create employment opportunities. Customs agreements permit the postponement of duty payments on imported goods, provide supplementary incentives relative to the standard tax regime, and offer financial support for expenditures in research and development, along with staff training. Madeira, due to its peripheral location and socioeconomic attributes, facilitated the creation of a free trade zone in the early 1980s. Poland possesses the biggest quantity of special economic zones, following Russia.

In Eastern Europe, besides the Russian and Polish experiences, Latvia presents two free zones, Rezekne and Liepaja, and two free ports, one located in the city, Riga, as well as in Lithuania and the Balkans region. We refer to Spain, which, along with the Free Zone of Vigo, encompasses the free ports and free trade zones of Barcelona, Cadiz, Las Palmas de Gran Canaria, and Ceuta. In compliance with European Union regulations, the Canary Islands have extended their offshore tax framework until 2026, subject to periodic renegotiation every 5 years.

Special Economic Zones, generally referred to as SEZs, are prominent in Europe, especially in the instances being analysed. The countries most comparable to Italy regarding socioeconomic structure have not undergone notable forms of special regions, but rather free trade zones (FTZs). Poland, Russia, and the Balkan nations, however, permit additional contemplation for labour development. Russia, despite lacking interventions for operations in SEZs, has profited from the high

Table 3.5 SEZs in Europe and Russia—summary

SEZ in Europe and Russia	Strengths and weaknesses
Poland	– Tax relief as the main form of facilitation, both for hiring and for investments and income taxes – Qualified and competitive workforce – Regulation of fixed-term contracts – Low wage levels, suboptimal working conditions – Incentive mechanisms provided at the end of the investment
Balkans	Macedonia: – Incentives for hiring that can be equal to 50% of the gross salary and for investment costs up to 50 million euros – Lack of qualified workers Bulgaria: – Possibility to transfer profits abroad without restrictions Serbia: – Skills shortage – Project on dual education (GIZ) Albania: – TEDA incentives are also provided for social security contributions and wages (150% deductibility for the first year); additional expenses for the same in subsequent years are deductible at 150%
Russia	– Qualified workforce – SEZ near universities and research centres

qualifications of the relatively small and low-cost labour resident in these zones, in comparison with foreign competitors. Poland has similarly prioritised workforce training; its available labour pool is greater than that of Russia, albeit less skilled. The integration of training and skill acquisition, along with comparatively consistent salaries, provides enterprises in SEZs with a significant competitive edge. The Polish Special Economic Zones exemplify how the creation of designated zones can positively impact unemployment reduction. In the establishment of SEZs in the tough region of the Balkans, the inadequately trained workforce emerged as a significant impediment to the operation of the special zone (Table 3.5).

References

Akinci, G., & Crittle, J. (2008). *Special economic zone: Performance, lessons learned, and implication for zone development* (Vol. No. 45869, pp. 1–83). The World Bank.

Böhmer, A. (2011). Key lessons from selected economic zones in the MENA region. First Meeting of the Working Group on Investment Zones in Iraq, Amman, 29–30 March 2011.

Brautigam, D., & Xiaoyang, T. (2011). African Shenzhen: China's special economic zones in Africa. *Journal of Modern African Studies, 49*(1), 27–54.

Cajati, R., & Gattamorta, E. (2010). *Governance: fattore chiave per lo sviluppo e la sicurezza in Africa*.

Ciociano, E., Berni, A., & Moschera, L. (2020a). Modelli Di Governance E Politiche Per Il Lavoro: Le Zone Economiche Speciali Nel Mondo. In L. Moschera & F. E. Caroleo (Eds.), *Le Zone Economiche Speciali: Aspetti Organizzativi E Di Policy. Vol. Annals Of Crisei* (Vol. 2). ISBN: 978-88-98279-10-4.

Ciociano, E., De Iudicibus, A., & Berni, A. (2020b). Analisi Della Governance E Delle Politiche Del Lavoro: Proposte Per Il Caso Campano. In L. Moschera & F. E. Caroleo (Eds.), *Le Zone Economiche Speciali: Aspetti Organizzativi E Di Policy. Vol. Annals Of Crisei* (Vol. 2). ISBN: 978-88-98279-10-4.

Farole, T. (2011). *Special economic zones in Africa. Comparing performance and learning from global experiences. Directions in development—Trade, n. 60059*. The World Bank.

International Labour Organization, (2015) "Key Indicators of the Labour Market" (KILM), ninth edition, 2015.

Kingombe, C., & te Velde, D. W. (2013). *Structural transformation and employment creation: The role of growth facilitation policies in sub-Saharan Africa. Background paper for the world development report 2013*. Overseas Development Institute.

Leong, A., & Pratap, S. (2011). *China's capitalist development and its implications for labour with special reference to the Shenzhen SEZ*. AMRC - Asia Monitor Resource Centre.

Newman, C., & Page, J. (2017). *Industrial clusters: The case for Special Economic Zones in Africa*. Wider United Nations University World Institute for Development Economics Research Working Paper 2017/15, Helsinki.

Ngai, P. (2004). Women workers and precarious employment in Shenzhen special economic zone, China. *Gender and Development, 12*(2), 29–36.

Remedio, E. (1996). *Exporting processing zones in the Philippines: A review of employment, working conditions and labour relations*. Economics Department, University of San Carlos, Cebu City, Philippines—ILO. Working paper n. 77, Geneva.

Reyes, R. (2011). *Latin American special economic zones and their impacts on regional security*. Thesis and Dissertation Collection, Naval Postgraduate School Calhoun: The NPS Institutional Archive, Monterey.

Vats, A., De Clerq, M., Clements, S., & Chen, X. (2018). *Special economic zones as a tool for economic development*.

Wang, J. (2013). The economic impact of special economic zones: Evidence from Chinese municipalities. *Journal of Development Economics, 101*, 133–147.

Wei, G. E. (1999). Special economic zones and the opening of the Chinese economy: Some lessons for economic liberalization. *World Development, 27*(7), 1267–1285.

Woolfrey, S., (2013). *Special economic zones and regional integration in Africa*. TRALAC—Trade Law Centre Working Paper n. S13WP10/2013.

World Bank, Worldwide Governance Indicators, (2018). https://databank.worldbank.org/source/worldwide-governance-indicators

Yeung, E., Lee, J., & Kee, G. (2009). China's special economic zones at 30. *Eurasian Geography and Economics, 50*(2), 222–240.

Yuan, Y., et al. (2009). *"China's First Special Economic Zones: The Case of Shenzhen*". A background study for the World Bank.

Zeng, D. Z. (2016). *Special Economic Zones: Lessons from the Global Experience*. PEDL - Private Enterprise Development in Low Income Countries PEDL Synthesis Paper Series n. 1.

Chapter 4
Special Economic Zones in Italy

4.1 Introduction

Established in 2017, SEZ in Italy aims to promote the growth of active firms and the establishment of new activities in the south of Italy by providing fiscal benefits, simplifying procedures, and securing customs permissions. The complexity of the implementation path delayed the launch of SEZ until 2021/2022. After the publication of the Law Decree 124/2023, the instrument has been profoundly changed by the establishment of a different type of zone for the entire South of Italy (ZES Unica per il Mezzogiorno).

Research has been undertaken during the instrument's inception and evolution. The examination of experiences from SEZs in diverse geographical regions has shown strengths and limitations pertinent to labour market analysis and the enhancement of employment growth. This study is advantageous for the future planning of targeted interventions in Italy, in particular in the Campania region. Despite the different experiences and settings analysed, which appear far from the Campanian context, several similarities and critical topics require attention.

In contrast to Italy, which possesses areas with unique fiscal characteristics, the notion of special economic zones remained unexplored until the enactment of the 2017 legislation that authorised their establishment. The previous chapter has provided a concise summary of special zones implemented in various countries. The objective is to identify policies, actions, and precedents that can assist in the formulation of governance for the SEZ in Campania and the development of its labour policies. We analyse the most significant examples of special zones that exhibit comparable characteristics and objectives to the countries under review and the designated regions of the SEZs, regardless of their success or failure.

Most studies highlight the emergence of SEZ in the world during the 1960s and 1970s, then its subsequent dissemination during the 1980s, and its significant acceleration during the 1990s and 2000s. Currently, there are approximately 6000 SEZs

A. Berni, *The Complex Environments of Special Economic Zones*,
SpringerBriefs in Economics, https://doi.org/10.1007/978-3-031-83425-7_4

in 140 countries, considering the estimated growth trend. Research has also demonstrated that SEZ areas worldwide have continued to develop because of international competition among governments, which is designed to attract continuously increasing investments to their territories. The review is helpful for both obtaining outstanding models and understanding potential issues that may arise from past experiences.

In recent years, scholars and researchers have shown increased interest in the creation of special economic zones (SEZs) as a viable strategy to increase investments, generate employment, and promote economic growth via tax incentives and economic benefits. Global experience demonstrates that interactions across diverse institutional entities (national and local governments, agencies, public and private organisations, etc.) are crucial for promoting innovation, advancing development, and increasing competitiveness. Although most of the research studies focus on the economic impacts of Special Economic Zones (SEZ), few investigate the effects of additional features such as management, governance, stakeholder roles, and the institutional framework on the sustainability of these designated areas. Therefore, it is essential to analyse the responsibilities of the members and the governance processes within the network since its creation (Berni & Moschera, 2019).

A fundamental attribute that allows us to classify a segment of territory as a special economic zone is the existence of a specialised governance framework. This is achievable by establishing an entity (or numerous entities with varying duties, degrees of autonomy, and operational capabilities) that can effectively administer the ‘special’ regime and ensure that both present and prospective investors may fully capitalise on its peculiar regulations (Farole, 2011). Therefore, establishing an effective and robust institutional framework is a critical determinant of success in any Special Economic Zone (SEZ). High-quality infrastructure, access to manpower, low-cost input elements, and appealing economic or financial incentives are often insufficient for many investors to establish themselves in a region.

The formulation of the SEZ’s regulatory scope and governance model must align with the characteristics of the SEZ proposal and the host country, which provides the operational framework for the SEZ.

The capacity of a nation to produce and maintain development is intimately linked to the efficacy of its governance. The World Bank defines a nation’s governance as the application of authority in the administration of social and economic resources for development. The notion parallels corporate governance, which delineates how a business administers its resources and allocates tasks and authority within its framework. In their eagerness to enhance attractiveness, numerous countries that have established Special Economic Zones (SEZs) devoid of a comprehensive governance model or institutional framework have inadequately considered that the political, bureaucratic, and social context, along with the governance model employed for the SEZs and its efficacy, are crucial determinants for attracting investments and maintaining a competitive advantage over time. Consequently, these nations have failed to achieve the development objectives established at the inception of the SEZs.

In specific instances, Special Economic Zones (SEZ) have functioned as a crucial 'laboratory' for the host country, generating new impetus for modifications to national rules and disseminating successful best practices from the SEZ to other institutional and bureaucratic frameworks (Vats et al., 2018).

The governance models of Special Economic Zones (SEZs) exhibit variability influenced by the specific characteristics and objectives of the zones, particularly in relation to the country's political system, the extent of centralisation or decentralisation at the territorial level (referring to the delegation of authority and responsibilities to public entities governing varying territorial extents, akin to the administrative divisions in Italy such as regions or provinces), the involvement of private entities in the strategic and operational management of the zones, and other pertinent factors.

4.2 The Impact of the Special Economic Zone on the Labour Market

A Special Economic Zone (SEZ) framework can implement diverse labour market initiatives, including targeted tax incentives for employment and programs for workforce training and retraining. Indeed, certain Special Economic Zones (SEZs) may provide authentic environments for testing innovative policies and developmental frameworks, particularly focused on addressing unemployment through labour legislation (Zeng, 2016). The implementation of effect assessment procedures for certain policies may be streamlined when confined to the parameters of the Special Economic Zone (SEZ), with the remainder of the country, where such policies are not enforced, serving as the counterfactual.

The impact of creating special areas, particularly for the labour market, can differ based on the various sorts of zones previously mentioned. The impact on employment will be markedly distinct and substantial in the context of a Special Economic Zone (SEZ) or an export zone, attributable to their broader geographical scope and economic sector diversification, whereas it may be less pronounced in the case of a business zone, restricted areas, or specific industrial parks.

The data on the employment proportion linked to SEZs, relative to the national total, indicate elevated figures for the Dominican Republic, Honduras, and Vietnam (30%, 30%, and 19%, respectively), as well as for Kenya (15%) (Farole, 2011). The ILO, conversely, offers data regarding the magnitude of employment in millions for the year 2008: In total, focussing just on the EPZs, employment rose from 22 million in 1997 to an estimated 66 million in 2006, with 40 million of those in China alone (Ahn, 2017). Ahn (2017) states that the SEZs accounted for roughly 0.21% of global employment in 2008 (Akinci & Crittle, 2008). Upon analysing the data by geographical regions, it is evident that the Asia-Pacific region (2.3%) and North and East Africa (1.59%) exhibit greater percentages. The percentage for the Americas is lower at 1.15%, with even lesser figures for Eastern Europe at 0.001% and sub-Saharan Africa at 0.20% (Table 4.1).

Table 4.1 Direct impact of SEZs on employment—Estimates based on ILO data. *Source*: Our elaboration on data from Akinci and Crittle (2008)

Geographical area	Employment (million)	Percentage of national employment (%)
Total	68.441	0.21
Asia and Pacific area	61.089	2.30
America	3.084	1.15
Western Europe	179	
East—Central Europe and Central Asia	1.590	0.00
Middle East and North Africa	1.458	1.59
Sub-Saharan Africa	1.040	0.20

The primary consideration about the effects of SEZs on the local labour market pertains to their capacity to influence the pre-existing market circumstances and, consequently, the potential advantages they offer, including job possibilities and working conditions. A successful SEZ generates direct employment, thereby providing static benefits to the labour market (Akinci & Crittle, 2008) and may be regarded as a potential catalyst for necessary structural economic reforms, serving as a model for other regions of the country or those with analogous characteristics and/or initial disadvantages. Nonetheless, the ephemeral character of the SEZ, functioning as a transitory rather than a structural remedy to labour market challenges, may diminish these advantageous elements. It functions as a safety valve for employment pressures amid elevated unemployment rates and diminishes the motivation to formulate and execute comprehensive reforms (Woolfrey, 2013). In an area such as Campania, where the unemployment rate is at 20.4% (53.6% for youth unemployment), a robust Employment Support Scheme would mitigate the issue by increasing job opportunities, provided it is not a transient measure (Eurostat data, 2019). The role of a 'safety valve' in high unemployment rates, frequently linked to extensive poverty, is largely attributed to the potential for foreign investment—an essential characteristic of Special Economic Zones—to provide increased labour demand. We do not underestimate the impact. The hunt for labour may occur within the local active population or in the investor's country of origin. Consequently, in the regulation of Special Economic Zones (SEZ), the discourse surrounding legislation related to foreign workers or individuals from regions outside the SEZ frequently ranks among the foremost goals of regulatory interventions. This is especially applicable to individuals from investing nations. It is crucial to acknowledge that foreign labour from investing nations and utilised in the SEZ is frequently allocated to managerial or highly skilled positions, thereby marginalising local workers who may be excluded from specialised professional opportunities with superior career prospects. It would not be analogous to the economic migration that has defined Campania in recent decades. The countries of origin and the degrees of specialisation may vary. In the region, Ukrainians, Romanians, and Moroccans are primarily engaged in precarious and low-skilled occupations, especially in family services, trade, construction, and agriculture. Specifically, they are utilised in sectors pertaining to families, business, construction, and agriculture.

The Special Economic Zones (SEZ), akin to the Export Processing Zones (EPZ), can function as a platform for young workers or individuals entering their first formal employment. In specific developing nations, there is a noted promotion of female employment, especially in contrast to the labour market beyond Special Economic Zones (SEZs). This phenomenon can be elucidated by the discernible inclination within Special Economic Zones (SEZ) to commence commercial operations that are predominantly labour-intensive and reliant on low-skilled labour, subsequently transitioning to a more technology-intensive framework engaged in sectors with elevated added value (COMCEC, 2017; Zeng, 2016). Some SEZ situations conduct targeted employment integration strategies for women, which substantially influence their empowerment and gender equality. (for instance, as occurs in Jordan).

Another factor to consider is the potential enhancement of the education system, vocational training, and on-the-job training resulting from the anticipated need for specialised skills by enterprises located in the SEZ.

A potential new training system, enhanced by the insights of international investors, may foster more rivalry, elevated standards, and an understanding of foreign markets that these companies introduce to local markets. This may render the area more susceptible to spillover effects that enhance the quality of the workforce and the human capital of the local labour force, as well as influence the technology employed (Kingombe & te Velde, 2013).

Nonetheless, it is feasible that polarisation arises among skilled worker groups, confined within the SEZ and not assimilated into the broader national economy and labour market. Furthermore, in the absence of suitable structural policies to facilitate growth, the implementation of new and superior technologies may result in technological progress without a corresponding rise in employment, or the opposite.

It is crucial to examine the impact of labour turnover in the SEZ as a conduit for the dissemination of technology and processes within the local economy, especially on the transfer of technology and managerial expertise to local enterprises. Certain nations have instituted non-renewable fixed-term contracts for local administrators in Special Economic Zones, with durations spanning from 2 to 5 years. In Shenzhen, China, the government employed these managers for a three-year term before mandating their departure from the region. As a result, numerous entrepreneurs have opted to establish their own enterprises, leveraging the experience acquired in the SEZs. This imposes competitive pressure on enterprises within the SEZ to innovate or become obsolete (Akinci & Farole, 2011). This feature could be incorporated into employment measures, serving both as a recommended best practice for investors and, more importantly, as a law for specific sorts of employment partnerships. This may be distinguished according to the competencies and the degree of specialisation needed.

The dynamic benefit of Special Economic Zones (SEZs) pertains to long-term, structural growth that is essential for the regional advancement of the respective area. They explicitly discuss the previously indicated impacts on growth, technical innovation, human capital, and national competitiveness (Table 4.2).

Table 4.2 Static and dynamic benefits. *Source*: our elaboration

Potential benefits	
Static benefits	Direct job creation
Dynamic benefits	Long-term development of a structural and regional nature (growth, technological innovation, improvement of human capital, increased competitiveness)

Many countries that establish Special Economic Zones (SEZ) have an underdeveloped welfare system or inadequate labour legislation. This indicates repercussions for the labour market regarding wage levels, the enforcement of workers' rights, and employment conditions, encompassing working hours, occupational safety, the right to strike, collective bargaining, safeguarding of union rights, parental leave, entitlement to sick leave, and access to a minimum of personal leave. Typically, we evaluate salary levels in SEZs against the national minimum wage or the remuneration in comparable sectors. The overall pay and benefits obtained by workers in Special Economic Zones (SEZ) are generally equivalent to or marginally exceed the income of comparable workers outside the SEZ (Farole, 2011).

EPZs represent a category of SEZs that often exhibit significant deficiencies in working conditions, likely attributable to the transient nature of employment in these zones. This impermanence diminishes the incentive for companies to invest in training and professional development, resulting in a low overall acquisition of skills. Certain Export Processing Zones (EPZs) delineate explicit standards for labour practices among the companies therein, concerning minimum wages, working hours, and conditions for union activities; however, these standards are frequently unenforced, and a limited number of EPZs have clearly specified the available inspection services to oversee labour standards. Although EPZ earnings frequently face criticism for being inferior to those in the external labour market, most studies indicate otherwise.

There exists considerable variation in salary disparities among enterprises both within and outside the zones. Typically, enterprises in the EPZs offer higher wages; nevertheless, there are cases where evidence indicates the contrary. The establishment of special regions generally results in a workforce reallocation effect, affecting both current employees and new recruits. The capacity to generate new jobs remains uncertain; nonetheless, when the EPZs possess considerable appealing attributes for the workforce, they can instigate large migratory trends, thereby impacting the associated local labour markets. The pressing issue of skills persists, frequently proving inadequate in meeting the requirements of the employment market. Most EPZs typically employ a higher number of women than men, but considerable variation exists among nations, facilitating increased female participation in the labour market despite the ongoing gender wage disparity.

The disparity between individuals employed within the SEZ and those outside it is notably pronounced regarding the consistency of contractual employment. The risk of employment in informal industries is, in fact, greater outside the SEZ than within it (Cirera & Lakshman, 2017). The informality of employment is a significant concern in the Campania region, and the SEZ is an opportunity to mitigate this issue. A 2016 study by the CGI of Mestre indicates that Campania's black GDP affects the official GDP by 8.8%, with an estimated 382,900 irregular workers.

The factors influencing overall working conditions differ according to the country in question, its ratification of ILO agreements, and the effectiveness of their implementation. Establishing Special Economic Zones sometimes entails complex situations, frequently involving nations that either partially or wholly uphold workers' rights. Notwithstanding efforts for enhancement, numerous issues persist unaddressed (Farole, 2011).

In many areas, despite labour legislation aligning with ILO recommendations, its implementation may be distorted, particularly due to insufficient labour inspections, prevalent worker intimidation, restricted access to special economic zones for third parties, and the corruption, control, or legal constraints imposed on unions by the institutions meant to safeguard them (Cirera & Lakshman, 2017; Cotula & Mouane, 2018). The safeguarding of workers' health and safety, the excessive work hours that violate permissible limitations, and the remuneration for overtime are frequently pivotal in the administration of labour relations in specialised zones.

The issue regarding industrial parks in Ethiopia is particularly pertinent, following an investigation by Le Monde that reported on research undertaken by the Stern Centre for Business and Industry at New York University. The study analysed the circumstances and remuneration of global workers, revealing that individuals in Bangladesh earn $95 monthly, those in Kenya $207, workers in China $326, and Ethiopians a mere $26. The analysis indicates that employees in the textile industry, predominantly women, receive inadequate training, endure deplorable working conditions, and experience very contentious interactions with the Asian management, marked by considerable cultural discord.

The investigation primarily concentrated on the Hawassa Industrial Park (South), one of five industrial centres opened by the government since 2014, employing 25,000 individuals and manufacturing apparel for global brands, with factories created by Chinese, Indian, and Sri Lankan enterprises.

The Ethiopian government has provided a tax exemption on profits for the initial 5 years of operation, as well as on the importation of machinery, capital goods, and numerous components to entice prominent corporations in the textile sector. It also permits the same foreign corporations to employ a substantial cohort of peasants as a labour force, reducing them to labourers for slightly over 20 euros a month. Aspiring employees from rural regions receive a dexterity assessment prior to employment, and their scores determine their placement in different manufacturing phases. Ethiopian legislation does not set a minimum wage for the private sector (public employees earn 420 birr per month, approximately 13 euros), enforces strict government control over trade unions, and requires any independent organisation monitoring working conditions to receive at least 90% of their funding from Ethiopian capital, effectively excluding Human Rights Watch, Clean Clothes Campaign, and other credible international NGOs. The work pace is frenetic, and employees from rural origins, predominantly women, lack housing accommodations. This situation differs from that of foreign personnel.

Employment in Special Economic Zones (SEZ) and Free Zones for Transformation and Export (ZFTE) frequently exemplifies harsh labour conditions (Roccella, 2010).

Although the SEZ gives a chance for development and employment growth, it is imperative to vigilantly prevent and monitor the risk of labour exploitation and the emergence of imbalances between internal and external labour markets. In certain nations, to avert anti-union practices or analogous circumstances, trade unions engage in negotiations with the management authorities of Special Economic Zones, exemplified by the Philippines, Singapore, and Trinidad and Tobago, where union representatives partake in the discussions (Akinci & Crittle, 2008).

The productivity of the local workforce and the management of labour relations significantly influence the appeal of a Special Economic Zone (SEZ) to international investors. The quality of skills and the productivity of labourers are critical for a region's sustained competitiveness. For this to persist, it is imperative that the labour regulations in place adhere to ILO standards, encompassing the principal rights of workers' assembly, organisation, and collective bargaining. Investors recognise the necessity of engaging in accordance with flexible and liberal labour market legislation. Concerning the employment regulations for foreign workers, enhanced openness is essential to mitigate undue dependence on foreign labour relative to local labour. The challenge is reconciling investors' requirements regarding free market dynamics and competitiveness with workers' rights. The possible effects of creating a Special Economic Zone on employment are neither clear nor consistent (Table 4.3). Demonstrating a significant impact of

Table 4.3 Special Economic Zones and labour market

Effects	
Job opportunity	Enhanced opportunities for employment resulting from the rise in job demand
Work conditions	Might change in relation to the previous conditions because of the implementation of ad hoc legislation for the SEZ It is possible to establish a different regulatory framework for the SEZ compared to regions outside of it
Women participation	Specific programs for female employees are frequently available
Informal economy	Special economic zones show a lower level of informality in the labour market compared to the external market
Professional training and education system	Enhancement is possible thanks to the expected demand for skills from enterprises located in the SEZ and the combination with innovations and knowledge introduced by international investors Regular ad hoc initiatives and collaborations between enterprises and educational training systems Risk of polarisation among skilled worker groups, limited to the SEZ and not integrated with the rest of the economy and labour market of the country Risk that the implementation of new and superior technologies, in the absence of suitable structural policies to foster growth, may result in technological advancement without a corresponding rise in employment, or the opposite
Spillover	Result from the comparison of employees and enterprises operating in the area
Technological advancement and investments in human capital	Overall effects, generated also by spillover and investments in training Short-term nature of these benefits poses a risk if not supported by structural measures

SEZ on the labour market is challenging due to the variability of findings in the research and the disparities among the nations analysed (Cirera & Lakshman, 2017; Zeng, 2016).

4.3 The Evolution of Special Economic Zones in Italy

Established in 2017,[1] SEZ in Italy seeks to foster the expansion of existing enterprises and the creation of new ventures in southern Italy by offering tax incentives, streamlining processes, and facilitating customs approvals. The intricacy of the implementation process postponed the debut of SEZ until 2021/2022. The issuance of Law Decree 124/2023 significantly modified the framework by creating a singular zone for all Southern Italy, referred to as ZES Unica per il Mezzogiorno. Decree-Law No. 124/2023 established the Special Economic Zone for the Mezzogiorno, referred to as 'ZES unica', effective January 1, 2024. This region includes Abruzzo, Basilicata, Calabria, Campania, Molise, Puglia, Sicily, and Sardinia. Eight unique administrative frameworks have supplanted the current Special Economic Zones.

The President of the Council of Ministers (DPCM) designated the eight SEZs via a decree that the Minister for the South and Territorial Cohesion is required to enact.

Regions classified as 'transitional' and 'less developed' possess the entitlement to propose the creation of special economic zones in compliance with European legislation.

Special Economic Zones (SEZs) and other regions with distinct tax regulations or comparable characteristics are not novel to Italy. The establishment of a designated zone aimed at fostering economic growth in disadvantaged or transitioning regions, particularly in the Centre-South, is exceptional. Prior to the DCPM of 2018, four regions adhering to the 'tax-exempt' plan may be identified (De Luca, 2017).

1. The Community Customs Code for free zones and warehouses delineates a specific regime for the Free Port of Trieste, the only free zone in the European Union. Vessels may berth at this port irrespective of cargo, destination, or origin and are immune from customs, taxes, or other costs save for service fees. Authorisation for disembarkation, embarkation, transshipment, handling, and storage is redundant, and there is no obligation to provide a customs destination for the items. Moreover, regulations concerning economic, health, and public safety issues delineate exceptions to the ban on customs interference during loading and unloading activities.

[1] On January 25, 2018, the DPCM adopted the regulation that established Special Economic Zones (SEZ). The DPCM ratified the GURI Serie Generale n. 47 on February 26, 2018.

2. Commodities from non-European Union countries can retain their foreign status at the Free Port of Venice without paying charges until an alternate customs destination is identified.
3. The Customs Agency designated the port of Gioia Tauro as a Free Zone on August 1, 2003, integrating simplified customs requirements that correspond with the deposit regime procedures. Entities qualified for the Free Zone at the port of Gioia Tauro can import goods from non-European Union countries into the EU, thereby accessing the national territory, without incurring taxes and with tax deferral.
4. The port of Taranto, including the Customs Free Zone, seeks to enhance efficient import/export activities that are duty-free for transactions conducted inside its limits.

Since 2013, the introduction of genuine special economic zones has been a focal point of legislative proposals, aimed at stimulating development in economically disadvantaged regions in the South and islands, with the goals of improving competitiveness, attracting foreign investment, and facilitating the movement of goods in the Mediterranean towards North Africa, China, and Suez. The SEZ was first formally created under the XVII legislature by the 'Southern Decree' (law decree of June 20, 2017, no. 91), which outlines its fundamental and formal features. This often includes locations such as ports, backport zones, productive and airport-related districts, logistical platforms, and interports, while excluding residential zones. Compared to existing free zones, special economic zones (SEZ) demonstrate greater complexity, indicating a variety of improved alternatives. The decree enables the establishment of interregional Special Economic Zones (SEZs), linking industrially focused areas of port less regions with neighbouring regions that possess ports. The SEZ may include non-contiguous regions within the same area, contingent upon a functional economic link defined by productive activities specified in the strategic development plan or adequate infrastructure connecting the regions, which must incorporate at least one port area. The latter must hold strategic importance for the territorial specialisation activities aimed at improvement.

On January 25, 2018, the Presidential Council promulgated a proclamation. Section 12 outlined the methodologies and legal stipulations for the establishment of Special Economic Zones (SEZs), including interregional SEZs, stipulating a duration of no less than 7 years and no more than 14 years, with a potential extension of up to an additional seven.

The regional president must submit proposals for the creation of a Special Economic Zone (SEZ) to the President of the Council of Ministers in accordance with European state aid regulations and the procedures outlined by regional laws. This submission should follow consultations with the mayors of the affected areas and include a strategic development plan that analyses the anticipated social and economic effects of the SEZ's establishment. Regions and prefectures establish specific protocols for control and monitoring operations to confirm legal compliance and create a monitoring plan that evaluates the effectiveness of initiatives.

4.4 Special Economic Zones in Italy: Proposal for Work

Decree-Law 91 of 2017 introduced the SEZ in Italy. Article 4 of the rule seeks to establish conducive conditions for the expansion of current companies and to encourage the establishment of new enterprises in certain sectors. The regulation presents multiple incentives for investors in SEZ zones, including both fiscal and non-fiscal advantages. The inefficiencies of the Italian logistics and port system serve as the foundation for understanding the setting up of the SEZ. A SEZ zone is described as a clearly delineated area within Italian territory that, although not required to be contiguous, must possess a functional economic connection. This includes a port area, as delineated by the community-level attributes specified in Regulation EU 1315/2013. The criteria for delineating the areas must adhere to the principles of the SEZ establishment regulation by considering existing infrastructures and those slated for enhancement, specifically including ports, retro port areas, inter ports, airports, logistics platforms, industrial zones, ASI areas, and PIP areas. Each SEZ was founded by a DPCM at the request of the relevant regions, accompanied by a strategic development plan in accordance with the procedures and criteria specified in Article 4, paragraph 3 of DL 91/2017. Thus, the prerequisites for the development of the SEZ include the existence of a minimum of one port region and its linkage to the trans-European transport network. As of December 31, 2023, there are 8 SEZ, comprising 6 regional/intraregional (Abruzzo, Campania, Calabria, Sardinia, Eastern Sicily, Western Sicily) and 2 interregional (Puglia–Molise, Puglia–Basilicata), with designated municipalities (or portions of them) identified for benefits.

In this perspective, SEZ represents a vital opportunity for the South and provides a different approach to government intervention. It no longer prioritises rain-like or predominantly supportive role but instead aims for a profound transformation in the developmental condition of the impacted regions. The transient nature of the SEZ is linked to its limited duration; nonetheless, the aim is to sustain its benefits in the region by cultivating skills and networks rather than merely focusing on labour and capital to enhance productivity and competitiveness (Lepore & Spirito, 2017).

The Svimez (2017, 2018) reports offer a critical evaluation of the economic conditions in the South. In 2017, the steady recovery continued amidst considerable uncertainty: GDP in the South increased by 1.4%, up from 0.8% in 2016, mostly propelled by a strong rebound in the manufacturing sector (5.8%) and, to a lesser extent, in construction (1.7%).

Regional performances exhibit variability: In 2017, Calabria, Sardinia, and Campania were the southern areas with the highest growth rates, at +2%, +1.9%, and + 1.8%, respectively. Between 2015 and 2017, the manufacturing sector witnessed a significant gain of 12.9%, while construction grew by 3.1% and services by 3%. Agriculture, however, is demonstrating a notable decline, registering a −4.2% reduction during the three-year period.

In 2017, employment in the South rose by 71,000, or +1.2%, whilst the Centre-North experienced a growth of 194,000 individuals. The duality in the Italian labour market persists, particularly when juxtaposed with the rest of Europe: both the northern and central areas conform to the European average, whilst the south lags by approximately 24 points. Furthermore, prolonged unemployment is rising in the South. The prevalence of long-term unemployment (12 months or more) is relatively unchanged in the Centre-North, although it rises by half a percentage point in the South, where the rates exceed those of the other region by more than three times.

Another thing to consider is the rise of NEETs nationwide. Caltanissetta (44.92%), Crotone (44.69%), and Palermo (40.39%) exhibit the highest NEET rates, over 40%. Regional study reveals that Campania has the largest prevalence of NEET individuals, exceeding 265,000 in 2017, followed by Sicily with 228,000, Lombardy with 173,000, Puglia with 142,000, and Lazio with 119,000.

The influence of migrant outflow on the population of southern Italy is a prominent phenomenon that receives less media attention than incoming movements, despite equal significance. The Italian population is experiencing significant structural changes, leading to a marked age imbalance that negatively impacts younger generations. In 2017, the Italian population reached 60 million, including 660 thousand inhabitants, indicating a decrease of approximately 106,000 from 2016, despite an increase in the immigrant population. In 2017, the Italian population decreased by 202,900, whilst the count of foreign residents rose by 97,400.

The Svimez report (2017, 2018) provides a thorough analysis of the demography of the South. The demographic importance of the South is steadily diminishing, presently at 34.2%, while the overall migration balance continues to be negative and is widening further. From 1976 to 2016, five million individuals migrated from the South to the Central-North, while three million returned, resulting in a net population decrease of two million in the region. In the last 16 years, 1,183,000 individuals have left the South. Fifty percent of those aged 15 to 34 are graduates; approximately 16% have emigrated, and almost 800,000 of them are unlikely to return to the South. Documents record the most significant exits from Campania, Sicily, Puglia, and Calabria. The principal aim is to secure Lombardy for Italy and to ensure Germany for EU members.

The analysis indicates that the strategic establishment of Special Economic Zones (SEZ) in pivotal logistics hubs has enhanced their performance in international relations. This decision has resulted in the acknowledgment of ports and logistics hubs as essential elements of productive communities. The cessation of extraordinary measures, the crisis affecting public enterprises, and a decline in available private capital for productive expansion have resulted in stagnation in the southern regions; however, the SEZs offer a potential avenue to re-establish the conditions requisite for structural economic recovery and the revitalisation of the local productive framework.

The succession of three governments since 2017 has already delayed the building of the SEZ due to its substantial potential to impact the labour market, and its success remains uncertain. In the context of employment, it is crucial to emphasise the ephemeral characteristics of the SEZ and the engagement of local workers, rather than the risks linked to the nations of potential investors. The efficacy of the regions will likely hinge on their capacity to foresee labour policies, which encompass not only tax incentives and contributions but also innovative and structural employment strategies. Discussions often revolve around exemptions to labour contract requirements; yet, this matter remains particularly delicate in Italy, potentially worsening the precarious circumstances of many workers and compromising their protections.

Thus, the active participation of social partners is crucial for executing suitable measures to tackle the current labour issues and the persistent employment crisis in the South. The areas included are Basilicata, Calabria, Campania, Molise, Puglia, Sardinia, and Sicily. Campania was the inaugural area to endorse Special Economic Zones and establish the official Steering Committee with all members in attendance. The following is a brief overview of the key employment measures suggested in the strategic plans for 2020 in the selected regions of the SEZ (Table 4.4).

Table 4.4 SEZ in Italy (2020): proposals for work in the Strategic Development Plans

Abruzzo	Decrease in employer-paid contributions on employee wages during the first years of operation Support of ongoing training to improve worker skills
Puglia	Incentives to employment and the enhancement of labour market participation, alongside strengthening of current regional policies N.I.D.I. initiative serves as a mechanism for the active labour policy of the Puglia Region Development goals related to sustainable and quality employment
Calabria	Quantitative and qualitative increase of the workforce, through retraining and education Introduction of school-work alternation processes throughout all sectors engaged with the marine economy, including ports, inland ports, and associated industrial zones Implementation of transport and logistics programs in high schools and higher technical institutes, focused on the key marine linkages of Calabria
Sardinia	Tax and contribution benefits Training and skill enhancement programs for employees
Sicily	Tax credit for training 4.0, which pertains to the tax credit for expenditures associated with employees participating in qualifying training activities, restricted to the company's costs corresponding to the hours or days of training Self-employment provides zero-interest loans to finance the initiation of modest entrepreneurial ventures undertaken by young NEETs Regulation for returning expatriates, a specialised framework established for workers—returning expatriates
Campania	Promotion of labour policy and enhancement of the employment services network to deal with unemployment Assistance for transitions (from employment to employment, from education to employment, etc.) Assistance for the enhancement and re-education processes within the framework of lifelong learning Enhancement of governance in the execution of labour policies Support for transitions (from employment to employment, from education to employment, etc.)

4.4.1 *Abruzzo*

The perimeter of the SEZ should include the areas of the ports of Vasto and Ortona, the former industrial consortia currently referred to as ARAP, and the Chieti-Pescara industrial consortium, along with the logistical hubs including Pescara airport, the Interporto of Manoppello, the Goods Distribution Centre of Marsica, and the truck terminals of San Salvo and Roseto.

In 2017, Abruzzo's macroeconomic environment showed moderate growth, with a GDP increase of 1.2% compared to the previous year. The enhancement is chiefly attributed to agriculture (+9% over the three-year period) and the manufacturing sector (+3.8%). The services exhibit a relatively moderate rise (+2%). Productive activity has increased in industry and services, but it has remained stagnant in construction. Employment has risen, leading to a reduction in unemployment rates, especially among young individuals. In 2010, the employment landscape worsened as both the labour force and unemployment rose. From 2015 to 2016, the work force showed slight growth, rising from 62.6% to 63.5%. The utilisation of highly trained labour is lower among regional companies compared to the national average. In 2016, despite a rise in the employment rate and a slight decline in the unemployment rate, the prevalence of long-term unemployment increased relative to 2011, attaining significant levels of 57% and 50.5%, respectively, although remaining below the national rate of 51.9% and the Southern rate of 58.4%.

Abruzzo's strategic development plan emphasises that rebuilding the business system is essential for restoring growth and regional employment levels. Moreover, it contends that territorially differentiated policies ought to complement the cohesion policy, which encompasses tax incentives, development contracts, and public investments, to improve the quality of vital public goods. The potential and specific incentives for employment encompass a reduction in company payments to employee wages during the initial operational years, alongside support for continuous training to enhance employee skills (Piano di Sviluppo Strategico ZES Regione Abruzzo, 2019).

4.4.2 *Puglia*

This area contains two Special Economic Zones (SEZ): the Adriatic SEZ and the Ionian SEZ. Initially, we anticipated that the newly established Special Economic Zone of the Southern Adriatic Sea would exhibit a polycentric structure, characterised by significant sectoral specialisation, robust internal cohesion and connectivity, both economically and logistically, as well as substantial physical and functional connectivity with one or more ports. Between 2008 and 2015, despite a net loss of 107,000 jobs, there was an increase in low-quality employment among both 'white-collar' and 'blue-collar' workers, impacting both male and female demographics, with around 56,000 new roles generated. In 2016, the area economy exhibited moderate growth, mostly attributable to the relatively favourable dynamics of industry and services bolstered by domestic demand. The promotional activities in SEZ-eligible areas encompass the creation of new agri-food supply chains (including fish and produce freezing, meat processing, ready-made meals, preserves, and fruit juices); the manufacturing of agricultural technologies (tractors, combine harvesters, etc.) and agri-food industry machinery (bottling machines, packaging machines, equipment for baked goods, etc.); and logistics, supported by the existing platform in the Incoronata area managed by Lotras. The enhancement of recreational watercraft building, automotive production, glass manufacturing, and aeronautics is essential.

The sectors listed below offer the most substantial opportunities for productivity and employment growth in the Adriatic region, dependent on the execution of appropriate investments with varying levels of intensity from Capitanata to Salento. The Puglia Region aims, pursuant to Subject Target VIII of the 2014–2020 Cohesion Policy, to promote sustainable and high-quality employment while enhancing worker mobility. The aim is to augment job availability by fostering employment and elevating labour market participation, while simultaneously strengthening current regional initiatives, such as further reductions in contributions, the enhancement and updating of professional skills, the encouragement of self-employment and entrepreneurial culture, the promotion of social cooperation, and suitable training for immigrants. The N.I.D.I. initiative functions as a proactive labour policy tool for the Puglia Region, promoting self-employment and entrepreneurship among women, the unemployed, precarious workers, those at risk of job loss, and youth; it offers assistance for business establishment through a non-repayable grant and a repayable loan for investment costs (Piano di Sviluppo Strategico ZES Adriatica, 2018). The Ionian Special Economic Zone is delineated as an interregional area located between Puglia and Basilicata. The targeted sectors include steel processing, shipbuilding, vehicle manufacturing and components, aviation, agricultural machinery, agri-food processing, contact centres, logistics, distribution activities, and e-commerce, namely the localisation of warehouses for multinational corporations.

The investments allocated for this SEZ will be capital-intensive. The development objectives correspond with the proposed measures of the Adriatic SEZ to attain sustainable and high-quality employment (Piano di Sviluppo Strategico ZES Ionica, 2018).

4.4.3 Calabria

Calabria's strategic strategy views the SEZ as a vehicle for sustainable growth, aimed at the import/export of industrially oriented districts connected to major transport infrastructures, providing incentives, services, benefits, and administrative simplification. Nonetheless, it functions as a mechanism for the regional government to promote the growth of productivity-oriented regions by applying the administrative simplifications and accelerations originally established in the SEZ to non-SEZ areas with considerable productive capacity, starting with less complex crisis zones. The primary sectors of the regional economy encompass agriculture, manufacturing, particularly light machinery, transportation, and warehousing. Calabrian employment rose in the first half of 2017 after a decline in the latter half of 2016, mostly within the service-based sector, particularly in trade and tourism. One of the many ambitious goals set by the Calabrian Special Economic Zone (SEZ) is the qualitative and quantitative improvement of the area workforce through retraining and education. This pertains specifically to initiatives that enhance training, fundamental and applied research, technical advancement, and innovative concepts. It encompasses targeted measures to promote education in logistics and transportation within elementary, secondary, vocational schools, and training centres, by utilising effective pedagogical methods and establishing specialised paths. It is essential to devise a strategy for the implementation of school-work alternation efforts throughout all sectors of the marine economy, encompassing ports, inland ports, and associated industrial zones. This entails the creation of transportation and logistics curricula in secondary and technical educational institutions, alongside initiatives that emphasise Calabria's vital connections to the maritime sector and related cultural endeavours, while considering the region's distinct attributes (Piano di Sviluppo Strategico ZES Calabria, 2018).

4.4.4 Sardinia

The Special Economic Zone of Sardinia should be characterised by an integrated 'network' framework encompassing coastal areas and the creation of free trade zones. The Sardinian labour market, although a slight decrease in unemployment, offers restricted opportunities, especially for highly qualified individuals. In 2017, there was a decline in permanent contract jobs and a rise in fixed-term contracts, but the unemployment rate remained approximately 17%. The focus will be on enhancing the food, metallurgical, and industrial sectors.

The establishment of training and reskilling programs for employees may coincide with the reduction of taxes and contributions (Piano di Sviluppo Strategico ZES Sardegna 2018).

4.4.5 Sicily

The Sicilian labour market has experienced significant enhancement over the last decade, with the jobless rate decreasing from 24.4% in 1998 to 12.9% in 2007. The positive figures about the unemployment rate stem from improved flexibility in contractual agreements and a rise in discouraged workers. The employment rate for those aged 15–64 is significantly low, at 44.6%, reflecting a lack of acknowledgment of human capital and a considerable proportion of inactive adults in this cohort, which is 48.8%.

The Strategic Plan of the SEZ Sicily Region (Piano di Sviluppo Strategico Zes Regione Sicilia, 2019) identifies Sicily's main specialisations as public administration services, education, and healthcare, in addition to real estate activities, whilst the manufacturing sector contributes a mere 7.8% to added value. The employment ratio in the sector illustrates Sicily's deficiency in industrialisation, with only 31 workers employed in the industry per 1000 residents, in contrast to the national average of 77.

It could be worth to consider two Special Economic Zones (SEZs) for Sicily: the eastern SEZ encompasses the provinces of Messina, Syracuse, Catania, Ragusa, and Enna, along with the southern region of Caltanissetta, whereas the western SEZ comprises the provinces of Palermo, Trapani, and Agrigento, in addition to the northern area of Caltanissetta. Decree-Law No. 34, issued April 30, 2019, titled 'Urgent Measures for Economic Growth and the Resolution of Specific Crisis Situations', advocates employment incentives for both Special Economic Zones (SEZs).

The tax credit for Training 4.0 is solely restricted by the company's expenses for training hours or days incurred during the relevant tax period. All businesses operating under the state's jurisdiction, irrespective of their legal structure, economic sector, size, accounting style, or income tax classification, qualify for this program. We distribute the financial help in the following manner: We designate 50% of the financial aid to small firms, capped at 300,000 euros per recipient; 40% to medium-sized enterprises, also limited to 300,000 euros; and 30% to large enterprises, with a maximum of 200,000 euros. Corporate or regional collective agreements must stipulate training days. The income tax return, contingent upon whether the investment is made by an individual or a legal entity, implements the provision for training expenses spent in the tax period following December 31, 2018.

SELF Employment offers interest-free loans to fund the initiation of small business endeavours pursued by young NEETs. Invitalia manages the funds under the Youth Guarantee Program, supervised by the Ministry of Labour and Social Policies. Financial resources are accessible for projects in all areas of goods manufacturing, service delivery, and commerce, encompassing franchising. This includes tourism (lodging, dining, and services), cultural and recreational services, personal services, environmental services, ICT services (multimedia, information, and communication), energy conservation and renewable energy, services for manufacturing and artisanal enterprises, retail and wholesale trade, and the processing and marketing of agricultural products. Nonetheless, if the aid amount is contingent upon the price or quantity of products that businesses acquire from primary producers or the market, or if the aid is predicated on a partial or total transfer to primary producers, it is inapplicable to businesses engaged in the processing and marketing of agricultural products. The Youth Guarantee initiative aims at young NEETs aged up to 29 who are neither employed nor engaged in educational or training activities. The program offers an interest-free loan to facilitate initial investments and management expenses. The loan amount ranges from a minimum of €5000 to a maximum of €50,000.

Individuals may commence self-employment and entrepreneurial endeavours by registering as sole proprietors, forming partnerships, establishing cooperatives with up to nine members, or creating professional associations and companies that have been inactive for no more than 12 months prior to the application date. The government has created a dedicated structure for the repatriation of expatriate staff. Commencing in 2020, new stipulations will be imposed on those relocating to Italy. The government has raised the income tax deduction from 50% to 70%, and subsequently lowered it to 90% for individuals relocating to Sicily. The regime streamlines entrance and broadens the facilitated regulations for individuals initiating a commercial activity on January 1, 2020. The government intends to extend enhanced tax benefits for an extra five tax periods, contingent upon specific criteria.

4.4.6 Campania's Special Economic Zone

In December 2016, the Campania Region approved the Regional Council decision about the Special Economic Zone, titled 'Project proposal for identifying areas for participation in the experimental phase of the Special Economic Zones promoted by the Government'. This decision specified the experimental SEZ regions in the ports and hinterlands of Naples, Salerno, Castellammare, and Bagnoli. On February 9, 2018, the Campania Region held a meeting with the appointed partnership after the public announcement of the Southern Decree and the Regulation on SEZs via D.P.C.M. no. 12. The consortium includes multiple entities, such as universities in Campania, ASI consortia for the provinces of Campania, Campano Interport spa, Southern Europe Interport, GESAC spa (responsible for airport services in Campania), Salerno Costa d'Amalfi Airport spa, Confindustria, Confcommercio, Assologistica, Anasped, Assiterminal, and the Port System Authority of the Central Tyrrhenian Sea. The meeting delineated the incentives accessible to firms and gathered feedback and suggestions for the construction of the strategic plan, an essential stage in obtaining the SEZ's recognition decree (Aniello, 2018). These are generic incentives and do not relate to labour market activities. The regional council ratified the strategic development plan by resolution (DGR) 175/2018 during the proposal phase, which also defined the governance of the SEZ. This DGR emphasises the importance of agreements with social partners, as the region promotes specific accords with local employer and worker organisations to formulate policies and development strategies for new initiatives in the SEZ, with the objective of enhancing employment and job prospects in these areas.

An advantage of the Campania Special Economic Zone is the swift communication between the coastal region and the interior, particularly between the port of Naples and the cities of Nola and Marcianise.

The SEZ is anticipated to fulfil substantial expectations: This offers a chance to rejuvenate the region's economy, based on a framework of structural intervention rather than sporadic and supportive measures, while recognising its ephemeral nature. Thus, it may be possible to eradicate central state interference in the South, characterised by extended emergency measures typical of the post-war period, by emphasising goals of competitiveness and professionalism.

Resolution number 720/2016 of the regional council suggested a complete 100% abatement of employer contributions on employee salaries for the initial 3 years of operation. Eligibility for this decrease is restricted to permanent contracts or fixed-term contracts with a minimum duration of 12 months. Should the periodic evaluations provide a favourable outcome, we may implement a 50% reduction for an extended term.

The Strategic Development Plan delineates the categories of workers targeted by the interventions, encompassing long-term unemployed individuals or those at risk of unemployment, workers experiencing crises, redundant employees lacking redeployment, and individuals susceptible to exclusion, including youth, women, and vulnerable or disadvantaged groups. The Pact for Campania executes the regional strategy targeting the 'youth' demographic.

The strategy must be founded on coordinated and integrated policies aimed at the local labour market, with two principal objectives: to enhance labour market activities that qualify and strengthen the active services of accredited operators, thereby improving their efficacy in boosting employability and employment; and to offer employment support for re-employing and retraining workers, maintaining employment levels, and facilitating job placement for individuals at increased risk of social exclusion.

The Strategic Development Plan outlines potential tools to prioritise for achieving these objectives, specifically promoting labour policies and strengthening the employment services network to reduce unemployment, including support for entrepreneurial initiatives; increasing women's workforce participation; enhancing governance in labour policy implementation; improving youth competencies to boost employability, thereby decreasing school dropout rates and fostering innovation and business competitiveness through internships and apprenticeship contracts; facilitating transitions (between jobs, from education to employment, etc.); supporting upskilling and retraining processes for lifelong learning; and cultivating territorial partnerships with the local stakeholder network. Most strategy plans lack thorough and systematic proposals for employment within the SEZs. Their main objective is to introduce tax and contribution incentives to promote hiring and training within the SEZ, while also leveraging established mechanisms, such as the N.I.D.I. initiative in Puglia and the SELF Employment program in Sicily, which is part of the Youth Guarantee plan. The Campanian strategic plan outlines criteria and primary goals. The occupational goals within the SEZ relate to labour market expansion and job assistance, improving existing labour policies, and optimising governance. Advocacy and facilitation of vocational training are essential strategies for enhancing employability, especially for adolescents, who must develop and hone their skills to facilitate the transition from education to employment. Although the administration's SEZ labour objectives are clear, it would be advantageous to specify the actions. The Calabrian idea, which directly addresses the future workforce (young students) by integrating school-work alternation with SEZ, is the most convincing and structured method. It also pertains to the existing workforce via retraining and training activities. A significant issue is the definition of activities aimed at developing skills beneficial in the SEZs. The main educational emphasis is on maritime economics and logistics. The reviewed materials offer minimal or no focus on the administration of foreign workers within the Special Economic Zones (SEZ).

4.5 Critical Issues: Insights for SEZ in Italy

Significant challenges discovered in other contexts may be relevant to the Campania SEZ. It is vital to use preventive strategies and analyse effective models as benchmarks (Ciociano et al., 2020). The most egregious adverse characteristics are the exploitation of individuals, the violation of fundamental rights, and unacceptable working circumstances. Many assessed countries have either dismissed, inadequately protected, or failed to implement the fundamental rights recognised by ILO conventions and international law. Ethiopia, India, China, Dubai, and Mexico are among the most prominent cases analysed. Therefore, it is essential to uphold a high degree of vigilance regarding the protection and execution of workers' rights, together with the enforcement of occupational health and safety regulations.

The sufficient presence, consistency, and frequency of inspection staff and controls within the SEZ largely guarantee adherence to the legislation. The principal risks of infractions in the Campania Special Economic Zone predominantly involve working hours and the lack of a legal employment contract, leading to undeclared labour and ensuing repercussions for labour protection, remuneration, contributions, and social security benefits (Ciociano et al., 2020). The worker categories necessitating the greatest protection due to increased risk encompass certain groups of vulnerable individuals: women, youth—especially those in their first employment—and international workers.

A Special Economic Zone must regulate the employment of foreign or migrant workers, even if its regulations differ from national migration policies. We will analyse the instances of China and Ethiopia, which illustrate the exploitation of migrant labour, even within the same country but in distinct regions, from rural areas to urban centres. Although special economic zones are highly beneficial for economic growth, they present a bleak situation concerning rights, especially for foreign or migratory workers. They often encounter discrimination in remuneration and career opportunities, hindering their potential for skill and pay progression. The regulation of migrant labourers is comprehensive, permeating both professional and personal domains, leading to modern forms of slavery and occasionally resulting in ghettoisation and marginalisation. One remembers the Chinese hukou or the emigration process. The drawback of foreign involvement occurs when foreign investors exert excessive control over firms established in the SEZ compared to the local workforce hired. Delegating critical positions to fellow nationals may disadvantage local employees seeking restricted prospects for career progression. In extreme instances, foreign investment can influence the cultural aspects and daily life of the host nation. The circumstances surrounding China's investment in Ethiopia are indicative. In the Campania region, it is crucial to evaluate professional mobility to guarantee equitable access to enhanced employment prospects for both domestic and international workers.

The analysis indicates that establishing sustained employment in the SEZ, consistent with essential workers' rights, is a challenging and praiseworthy goal. This indicates that the employer in the SEZ ought to receive fair compensation, access to training and professional development, and obtain enough or new capabilities for their responsibilities. Compensation should consider the employee's educational qualifications and training proficiency. If this individual undergoes retraining or enhances their skills or knowledge, it is essential that their salary or wage correspondingly reflects this advancement, thereby motivating an increase in productivity. We must avoid the situation in Poland. Often, when an individual improves their skill set, they may not experience a corresponding increase in their compensation.

The utilisation of fixed-term contracts constitutes another significant facet of the inquiry. Fixed-term contracts inherently possess no negative connotation and function as a versatile tool to meet labour requirements, rendering them suitable for use in particular sectors. However, due to its generation of precarious and transient employment, its application must not descend into exploitation. Therefore, it is crucial to include a synergy with preventive actions targeting widespread precariousness into the design of tools for the Campania region.

Among the assessed specific regions, several have been identified as outstanding, especially concerning the design and implementation of targeted employment interventions. The assessment of employment outcomes is unclear, especially concerning training and skills, equal opportunities, youth employment, and the mitigation effects of informal employment plans.

Botswana has instituted training and employment regulations within the SEZ relevant to the primary sectors of the national economy. Training is an essential catalyst for the success of the distinctive zone. This explains the existence of not only fundamental ad hoc and sector-specific training programs but also a network of committed participants engaged in the training and education of future workers in the SEZ or those who are already potentially active inside it. Based on the idea of using international experiences for domestic implementation, universities, high schools, and research centres actively engage in internationalising education because they view international benchmarking as a critical element for improving the national workforce. This may correspond with or augment the imperative to attract foreign investments, an essential and foundational element in the characterisation of a Special Economic Zone (SEZ). The uniform design guarantees consistency between educational institutions and the professional domain.

The shift from education to job is more adaptable, and overseeing students during mandatory schooling is more uncomplicated, which is a vital element in tackling school dropout rates.

The plan detailed in the Strategic Development Plan of Calabria is equally persuasive, like the initiative in Botswana, as it involves the participation of diverse stakeholders in education and training. The ability of students to transition between education and employment, the involvement of higher technical institutions, and the scheduling of training to align with the primary industries in the Calabrian Special Economic Zone—particularly logistics, with an emphasis on port logistics and maritime-related enterprises—make this particularly simple.

Another training method to consider is in-house training, as noted for Cambodia, which takes place within the specific manufacturing organisation and is, in some respects, more flexible and economical than external training.

Alongside the previously mentioned working conditions, it is essential to highlight a significant benefit of the Ethiopian Special Economic Zones: the establishment of a specialised textile processing centre, intended to function as a centre of excellence for enhancing all phases of the production cycle. To improve the quality and competitiveness of the final product and to attract a broader spectrum of professionals, including highly specialised researchers and those who perform more straightforward tasks, it is imperative to establish specialised centres that concentrate on the most prospective productions in the region.

Spillover effects and knowledge transfer in neighbouring producing areas can enhance human capital, acting as a catalyst for the development of the Special Economic Zone. This is a characteristic aspect of industrial areas, as demonstrated in Panama, where the arrival of foreign immigrant labour has enabled the cultivation of a skilled workforce. The enhancement of the existing workforce and the integration of marginalised groups into the labour market is a goal of the SEZ, consistent with the wider labour market in Campania that exists beyond the special area, as employment conditions for women and youth are notably precarious in the region. Consequently, it may be prudent to contemplate the implementation of targeted strategies for the integration of these groups within the SEZ (Ciociano et al., 2020).

Regarding women's employment, it is crucial to recognise the concept of empowerment, a process that transforms power dynamics in various societal and personal situations, contesting the subjugation of women by men and fostering equality. It emerges in three dimensions: individual and psychological, organisational and socio-political, and community; thus, it is apparent in the workplace concerning compensation opportunities and career advancement. This transcends the mere establishment of equal opportunity as a manifestation of the Constitution's principle of equality; it further elevates women's positions in society and within the family structure. This is important not only for transitioning economies but also for the Italian context, especially in the South, where women's professional and social participation does not regularly and fully occur without specific conditions (such as childbirth).

Jordan, Ethiopia, and Mexico illustrate the essential function of the workforce in the development of specialised areas and compliance with labour standards.

The outcomes of individual women's employment initiatives in Jordan are crucial for the overall success of the specified region. They offer a chance to elevate women's status, alleviate familial poverty, and reduce job informality.

Women, constituting most of the workforce in the textile sectors of Ethiopia and Mexico, spearheaded the protests labour abuse. Absent the protestations of these individuals, the horrible working circumstances they endure would probably remain concealed. The criticism has sparked a discussion on the necessity of sustainable consumption and production, particularly in relation to the textile sector. In the Campania region, it is imperative to tackle youth unemployment and execute appropriate actions to alleviate this issue. In South Africa, labour initiatives in the Special Economic Zones (SEZs) principally seek to mitigate youth unemployment through the implementation of targeted incentives and regulatory measures that ensure the effective use of these resources for the recruitment of young adults. The prevalence of informal employment is a widespread characteristic in various contexts, irrespective of their severe poverty and evident disconnection from the economy and society of Campania.

The struggle against unreported labour commences with the promotion of employment formalisation. This can be achieved by reducing labour costs, executing informational campaigns, ensuring payment traceability (as evidenced in Jordan, where we have implemented payment digitisation to discourage irregular employment relationships), and instituting a comprehensive control system to verify labour compliance within the SEZ.

The establishment of offices dedicated to people management and organisation within the SEZ is a compelling proposal to contemplate. One may either establish them anew, as Nigeria has accomplished, or restructure the current public administration departments. At this stage of the study, it is essential to understand the strategies that may be implemented to prevent significant problems and enhance the probability of success. Based on an examination of Italy's and Campania's present active and passive labour policies, we develop the recommendations for labour market interventions in the SEZ to accomplish this goal. These recommendations are in keeping with the employment goals specified in the Strategic Plan of Campania.

Table 4.5 summarises the concerns articulated to date, illustrating an evaluation of possibilities and dangers alongside strengths and weaknesses (Table 4.6).

Table 4.5 Proposal for special economic zone in Campania

Weaknesses	• Worker exploitation and the potential for unregistered employment • Rights violations • Management of foreign labour: mitigating discrimination • Regulation of foreign investors: preventing excessive monitoring of the labour force • Unfair remuneration • Misuse of fixed-term contracts
Strengths	• Network for training and education • Training and education for primary economic activities • Incentives for training, including in-house programs establishment of specialised hubs • Incentives and customised tools for youth and women • Addressing undeclared work with focused on solutions • Dedicated employment offices in SEZs

Table 4.6 SEZ and labour policies: SWOT analysis

Internal factors	Strengths	Weakness
	– Incentives for training (including in-house types) – Establishment of highly specialised hubs – Incentives and tailored tools for youth and women – Working conditions may change compared to the pre-existing situation due to the adoption of specific laws for SEZs special offices for work in the SEZ Labour market within the SEZ is more informal than that of the external market	– Worker exploitation and the potential for unreported employment – Rights violation – Unfair remuneration – Misuse of fixed-term contracts
External factors	Opportunities	Threats
	• Network for training/education • Training and education for predominant economic activities • Technological innovation, investments in human capital. Overall effects, generated also by spillover and investments in training • Dynamic benefits (long-term structural and regional development: Growth, technological innovation, improvement of human capital, increased competitiveness) • Static benefits (direct job creation)	Different regulatory system may be established compared to areas of the country outside the SEZ Management of foreign investors Risk of the temporary effects of the SEZ if there are no accompanying structural interventions Vocational training and education system: Risk of polarisation among skilled worker groups

References

Ahn, P. (2017). Global trends in EPZs/SEZs. ILO Workshop on Employment Relationships, Workers Rights, and International Experiences on TU Movement and Campaigns on 2 March 2017 at UNCC, Bangkok, Thailand.

Akinci, G., & Crittle, J. (2008). *Special economic zone: Performance, lessons learned, and implication for zone development* (Vol. No. 45869, pp. 1–83). The World Bank.

Akinci, G., & Farole, T. (2011). *Special economic zones - Progress, emerging challenges, and future directions*. International Trade Department Investment Climate Department, World Bank.

Aniello, V., (2018). Zone Economiche Speciali e Zone Logistiche Semplificate. Misure per lo sviluppo dei porti ed elementi per una valutazione di impatto. Documento di ricerca, Fondazione Nazionale dei Commercialisti, 30 maggio 2018.

Berni, A., & Moschera, L. (2019). Dealing with complex environments: The case of special economic zones in Italy. In *Knowledge ecosystems and growth: 14th international forum on knowledge asset dynamics - IFKAD 2019*. IKAM—Institute of Knowledge Assets Management. ISBN: 978-88-96687-12-3.

Ciociano, E., De Iudicibus, A., & Berni, A. (2020). Analisi Della Governance E Delle Politiche Del Lavoro: Proposte Per Il Caso Campano. In L. Moschera & F. E. Caroleo (Eds.), *Le Zone Economiche Speciali: Aspetti Organizzativi E Di Policy. Vol. Annals Of Crisei* (Vol. 2). Fondazione Nazionale di Ricerca dei Commercialisti E.T.S. ISBN: 978-88-98279-10-4.

Cirera, X., & Lakshman, R. (2017). The impact of export processing zones on employment, wages and labour conditions in developing countries: Systematic review. *Journal of Development Effectiveness, 9*, 1–17.

COMCEC. (2017). Special economic zones in the OIC region: Learning from experience. In *Standing Committee for Economic and Commercial Cooperation of the Organization of Islamic Cooperation*. Coordination Office.

Cotula, L., & Mouane, L. (2018). *Special economic zones: engines of development or sites of exploitation?* Briefing IIED, October 2018.

De Luca, R. (2017). *Le Zone Economiche Speciali: caratteristiche, agevolazioni, opportunità e aspetti operativi. Documento di ricerca*. Fondazione Nazionale dei Commercialisti. 31 gennaio 2017.

Eurostat. (2019). Dati sull'occupazione in Europa

Farole, T. (2011). *Special economic zones in Africa. Comparing performance and learning from global experiences. Directions in development—Trade, n. 60059*. The World Bank.

Kingombe, C., & te Velde, D. W. (2013). *Structural transformation and employment creation: The role of growth facilitation policies in sub-Saharan Africa. Background paper for the world development report 2013*. Overseas Development Institute.

Lepore, A., & Spirito, P. (2017). Le Zone Economiche Speciali: una leva di politica industriale per lo sviluppo manifatturiero e logistico del Mezzogiorno. *Rivista giuridica del Mezzogiorno / a., XXXI*(4), 855–967.

Piano di sviluppo strategico ZES Calabria. (2018).

Piano di Sviluppo Strategico ZES Regione Abruzzo. (febbraio 2019).

Piano di Sviluppo Strategico ZES Sardegna. (novembre 2018).

Piano di Sviluppo Strategico ZES Sicilia. (agosto 2019).

Piano di Sviluppo Strategico ZES Adriatica. (agosto 2018).

Piano di Sviluppo Strategico ZES Ionica. (agosto 2018).

Roccella, M. (2010). La condizione del lavoro nel mondo globalizzato fra vecchie e nuove schiavitù. Ragion pratica, Rivista semestrale, Il Mulino, 2/2010, 419–438.

Svimez. (2017). *Rapporto Svimez 2017 sull'economia del Mezzogiorno. Introduzione e sintesi*. Svimez. 7 novembre 2017.

SVIMEZ. (2018). Rapporto Svimez 2018. L'economia e la società del Mezzogiorno, il Mulino.

Vats, A., De Clerq, M., Clements, S., Chen, X. (2018). Special Economic Zones as a Tool for Economic Development.

Woolfrey, S. (2013). *Special economic zones and regional integration in Africa*. TRALAC Trade Law Centre Working Paper n. S13WP10/2013.

Zeng, D. Z. (2016). *Special Economic Zones: Lessons from the Global Experience*. PEDL - Private Enterprise Development in Low Income Countries PEDL Synthesis Paper Series n. 1.

The manufacturer's authorised representative in the EU is Springer Nature Customer Service Centre GmbH, Europaplatz 3, 69115 Heidelberg, Germany. If you have any concerns regarding our products, please contact ProductSafety@springernature.com

Printed and bound by CPI Group (UK) Ltd, Croydon, CR0 4YY
01/10/2026
02225981-0006